VOICE OF GOD

JOSEPH Z

Contents

Prelude

It was an early autumn morning in Minnesota; the sun was barely breaking the horizon. The Voice of God had drawn me to the edge of a freshly tilled field by way of a short, wooded path not far from home.

He asked me, "What do you see?"

I paused, then said, "A plowed field." I calmly turned to walk away. His voice came again, saying, "Go back and look."

I replied, "Yes, Sir." I spun back around, once again standing at the end of the short, wooded path. Looking intently across this normal-sized field, there were no more questions. Instead, a statement welled up inside of me with peace and assurance.

"As far as your eyes can see, I have called you to reach the masses and build lives by the Word of God."

I was flooded with a deep knowing that the Voice of God had spoken to me. Suddenly, my mind opened to the image of millions of people in this field and beyond.

A relaxed intensity came over me, and I again submitted to His Voice, "Yes, Sir."

"...that the word of the Lord may run swiftly and be glorified, just as it is with you." – 2 Thessalonians 3:1

Chapter One

Voices On The Wind

The summer days of my childhood were filled with farm work and recreation. A high point of any given day would be to finish my responsibilities while leaving enough free time for an adventure. This usually entailed long walks, climbing, building tree houses and hunting on our large wooded property, accompanied by my main companion, my German shepherd, Duke. It was thrilling for me to be autonomous and out of reach.

In my youth, I discovered an attraction to the quietness. Being far removed from everything awakened my creativity and caused my imagination to grow. These times of recreational solitude were very enjoyable, and they produced an internal, peace-laden stillness. Off-roading on my ATV, hunting, and building tree houses were some of the happiest times in my young life.

Duke and I would often hike through the vast property, stalking grouse near the banks of the broad river, which ran miles alongside the property. It was during these times that a unique thing would happen. I seldom mention it because there has never been an easy way to explain the experience.

Yet, over time it seemed to occur more frequently. The experiences weren't startling, but they certainly piqued my curiosity: a voice calling my name from a distance, seemingly travelling with the wind over the treetops with a distinctly familiar sound. Much like an echo, although twice as loud—loud enough to be heard clearly—but in the form of a distant shout. Most of the time, the shout would sound very much like the voice of my dad.

One day, after mistaking this voice for my dad's, I drove my ATV to find him back at the house. After asking him what he wanted and why he called me, he replied, "I didn't call you."

This was very strange to me, yet, I knew to never question my dad. This scenario actually developed into a somewhat regular occurrence.

Another time, after finding my dad—thinking his voice had been summoning me—he admitted something that I will never forget.

He asked me, "Did you hear someone call your name?"

"Yes."

"Did it sound like I was calling you?"

"Yes," I replied again.

Smiling, he said, "I know. I have had that happen to me as well."

That was the last time we directly spoke of it. I didn't really know what to do with this mystery, nor dad's response to me about it. As a result, it was left as a strange family understanding and treated like no big deal.

Psychology uses the term "normalcy bias". Something so strange and out of place occurs, but everyone subconsciously ignores it and goes on with life as usual. This was the case regarding this situation and my family. If it ever did come up in the slightest reference, it was wry and a little humorous, then dismissed as quickly as it came up.

After this conversation with my dad, it happened again, but this time it was frightening.

I had stepped off my ATV and began looking over a half-mile-long field. This was one of those moments that was meant for me to enjoy the peace and stillness that ignited creativity and imagination. Duke and I were positioned about a football field length from the tree line behind us.

The stillness was beautiful but was starkly broken by the shout of my name. Once again in the distance, but out over the open field in front of us. After listening for a moment, I called back, "Yeah?—What?!"

Silence. For a moment, my attention turned to Duke, but then the voice came again, "JOE!!!!"

Now it was closer—a lot closer! As I stood next to the ATV, I called back again, "What?!"

Again, there was no sound, no voice calling. Then Duke's hair began to rise. As the hair on the nape of his neck bristled and stood tall all along his back, his demeanor changed into an intent stare.

Suddenly, I heard the same voice, yet it was no longer a shout, and no longer from far away: it was slightly above a whisper and within arm's reach.

Duke flinched, laid his ears back, and ran away as fast as he could. This was not a typical response—he was a courageous dog!

For example, one day our Charolais bull became enraged while I was in the pen. As he was pawing the ground, preparing to charge in my direction, I took on a baseball stance, as if to steal a base. Having nowhere to run, I was preparing myself for an attempt to dodge the charging bull.

Yet, before he could get to me, Duke jumped through a nearby fence and violently attacked him, allowing me to narrowly escape. So, when Duke—my loyal, brave companion—ran from the voice in fear, it really got my attention!

My response was nearly equal to his, both in fear and speed! I jumped on that ATV and drove away as fast as I could. In my mind, there was no need to investigate or engage whatever was happening. That experience, along with many similar encounters, caused a great deal of fear in me as a young person, to the point of becoming something I had to deal with as an adult.

In addition to hearing distant voices outside, my world at that time was filled with supernatural encounters, such as my bed shaking and seeing entities appear in my room. Unfortunately, these occurrences were somewhat regular, and it was terrifying.

Beyond Voices

Even beyond just hearing voices, I had other strange experiences as a boy. Unique moments would periodically happen, but they never seemed out of the ordinary to me because they were common.

For example, one day while watching TV, I "zoned out" (for lack of a better term). This makes me laugh writing it because anyone who has children will say, "Yeah, we see that all the time!"

However, this was different.

Not long before this day, my dad had taken me to see *Rocky III* in the theaters. So, there I was, laying on the floor with my hands supporting my face, subconsciously watching TV, and simultaneously daydreaming about the third Rocky. Then I saw a snippet of a movie trailer for the next film. I saw a big Russian and read the title, *Rocky IV*.

I thought this new movie looked pretty cool, so I decided to tell my family about the trailer I'd seen. In a matter-of-fact tone, I conveyed, "Rocky is going to fight a Russian in the next Rocky movie called *Rocky IV*." Not knowing the plot, just a very simple theme from the images I had seen, I continued, "Apollo Creed will have to train him again, because his old trainer, Mickey, died."

I don't remember who, but one of my family members said, "Umm, *Rocky III* just came out. You don't know who he is fighting in the next movie, or even if there will *be* another movie."

It hadn't even occurred to me that I couldn't have known if there were plans to make another movie, as *Rocky III* was still in theaters. A new trailer for *Rocky IV* couldn't possibly have existed yet!

Yet, while I had watched TV, my imagination had transformed from a simple daydream into a brief moment of watchable information, in the form of a short movie trailer, that no one else in the room witnessed. It wasn't necessarily spiritual or spooky; it was just information in the context of something I was thinking about.

Interestingly, this hadn't even been a big deal to me because it seemed so normal. It was like a sharp picture in my mind, only like I was viewing it on the outside. In fact, I actually thought I had seen it on the TV.

It's hard to recall how I responded at the time, in the face of my family's disbelief. What I do know is that this experience was a supernatural prediction shown to me a couple of years in advance of any news or movie preview for that film. This stands out in my memory because both family and kids at school just shrugged it off when I said, "Rocky will be fighting a Russian." Yet, I knew with my heart that it was true. Sure enough, a couple of years later, Rocky fought a Russian in *Rocky IV*.

This moment wasn't something I made happen, and the many moments like it afterward never came with warning either. The relevance of these events became enlightening to a degree; they showed me that regardless of whether people believed what I said or not, my experiences were real.

Still, after these episodes, and not being understood, I decided to simply hide most of these encounters in my heart. It was a significant discovery that when I was very relaxed and thinking about something specific, information would sometimes come to me.

The information was most often related to what I was thinking about. It would come in different ways, such as seeing it, or having an intuitive knowing about it, in a present, past or future tense, as though the information had been told to me by someone.

As time went on, I learned that there are certain times, when I look at someone or something long enough, information will begin to come to me about them, often in an emotional way. This type of experience gave me a heightened sense of empathy, which caused me to be introverted to a degree, especially when meeting new people.

My close friends would never have thought of me as an introvert. However, it was because of knowing them and no longer experiencing what I now call "traffic"—the feelings or impressions I would get from them. The closer I got with people, the less I "felt" things from them.

It was not easy to walk around like a radio antenna! I remember going to the funeral of a lovely aunt of mine who had died of cancer. At her burial, we were all gathered around her casket, and there was a reading of her journal entries during her last days.

As they read it, I suddenly felt as though I was in her room with her, experiencing her pain and hopelessness. Being very young, there was no way for me to process what was happening. I began to weep violently, which was not common in our family, and it must have embarrassed my dad. I was overcome because I was directly experiencing her feelings, and I couldn't avoid it.

No reprieve led to tears of anguish and a sensation of tormenting sorrow. It was a horrible thing to feel at that age—someone dying—and the darkness that can enter a mind and heart was unbearable. The imagery of her torment was in full color inside of me. I could see her looking around her room at times, finding no one to bring relief. All I could do was sob.

One of my cousins came up to me after the service and said, "Wow, that really hit you hard, huh?" Being just young kids, there wasn't a way of articulating what was happening to me. So, she just hugged me and said, "It will be ok." The weird thing is that during this experience, I felt like a bystander. It wasn't that the scenario was so sad; it was that I ran into the traffic of her emotions and memories through hearing her journal being read.

My response to that season of random encounters was to head back to the woods, back to farming, back to hunting with Duke, and doing my very best to just enjoy peace and creativity. However, these encounters were only the beginning. The Voice of God impacted my life then, and the journey continues to this day.

Chapter Two

My Ultimatum

In the previous chapter, I talked about encounters that I had as a young person. I had a lot of scary and intriguing things happen as a boy. However, all of that changed when I entered a born-again relationship with Jesus.

Things didn't change in the way you might think. When I gave my life to Jesus, rather than supernatural encounters calming down, the very opposite happened! It was as if the decision to follow Jesus woke something up inside me, causing those experiences to significantly increase. Suddenly, it seemed as though I had entered into a season where the supernatural followed me everywhere. During this time, things in my family also became very intense.

Everything in my young life culminated in the fork in the road when I decided to follow Jesus. I was given an ultimatum, with consequences that hinged upon whether I was going to stand on my newfound decision to follow Jesus or not. This choice culminated in what was (at the time) a very costly exchange.

Backstory

My mom and dad got divorced when I was a toddler. There was violence and many other challenging issues involved. As a result, they had joint custody of me and my two younger siblings. We would see my dad Tuesdays, Thursdays, and every other weekend. In the summer months, our parents would take turns with us every other week until school started again.

Dad was a guidance counselor and state champion football coach for a nearby school. On his nights with us kids, he would pick us up on his way home from work. During these evenings, he would sit down with a coke and brandy and spend hours helping me with my homework. He was very dedicated and consistent in his desire to see all of us excel in school.

My dad was a man's man with a solid build, six foot two inches tall, and an explosive personality to go with it. He was hard working, very educated and excelled at his career in teaching, counseling, and coaching. He did all this in addition to running a profitable Charolais cattle farm and various land investments. Because of his profession, he naturally placed a high priority on education, sports, and physical fitness.

For example, one afternoon, he and I were working in the garage. I said, "Dad, I would like to learn karate." In response, he simply walked over to two 2x4 boards leaning against a wood-burning stove. He halfway took a knee and punched the bottom of these 2x4s near the floor, instantly breaking them both! He said, "You don't need karate; you just need muscle." So, I never brought it up again. That was his mentality toward many things.

Hostility Toward Religion

Dad had a negative view of religion, especially anything of a spirit-filled persuasion. From what I understand, he experienced some nasty things many years before. His father was also hostile toward anything that had to do with a spirit-filled religious experience. My grandfather lived on the same property and was also a teacher. He played the accordion, drank brandy, and ran the cattle farm with my dad. He and my dad had both made the record books at the University of Minnesota for college football. In fact, in his youth, my grandfather had been offered a professional sports contract with the NY Giants.

There is a tragic segment of my grandfather's early life involving a younger brother whom he used to carry on his back because his legs didn't work. One day, someone in the family made a passing comment to me that Grandpa had asked God to help his brother. Unfortunately, his brother died shortly after. There is no way to verify the exact scenario, but I suspect that this was possibly one of the roots of anger toward any belief that God does miracles today.

My Grandfather liked me but was negative any time the topic of spirit-filled religion came up. The atmosphere between my dad and grandfather demanded mockery of anything miraculous or involving the power of God. Truthfully, I had even participated in this mockery as a youth to gain their approval.

I only ever heard bits and pieces from my dad regarding his negative opinion of religion. I suppose that it may have been rooted in my Grandfather's loss; therefore, causing him to reject any notion that God moves miraculously. Part of my dad's story, as it was told to me, was that my dad had gone to a spirit-filled meeting of some kind and had a touch from

God. However, when he returned home to tell my grandfather about it, his response was profoundly belittling. Whatever my dad had encountered (real or not) was crushed.

Now, the fact that my mom was taking us to a church that believed in the power of God definitely did not ease his position. Whatever the deep-rooted cause of his hostility toward spirit-filled believers, there is one thing I do know for sure: it always made my dad livid anytime the topic of religion was mentioned. Understandably, I avoided the religion subject as much as possible, especially anything to do with a spirit-filled persuasion.

I have a vivid memory of my dad laughing loudly and mocking Jimmy Swaggart when he went on TV crying and apologizing for his failures. My dad was also adamant regarding TV preachers, often stating, "The saddest thing in the world is old people with no hope sending these fools all their money."

He was so dedicated to driving the point home to me about how stupid the people at my mom's church were, that he would sit with me and mock every person pictured in her church directory. He called it "Mad Magazine," which I thought was pretty funny.

To this day—regardless of the mockery, violent outbursts, and consistent anger—many things about my dad genuinely make me smile. He was a legitimately funny person and so quick-witted!

Aside from all that, I know he loved my siblings and me, and we loved him, too. I still do, today. This man, with all of his faults and antagonism toward the church, would have protected me with his dying breath. In elementary school, I got into a fight on the school bus with two or three guys who were bigger than me. Not just a little bit bigger, either. These guys were in 11th and 12th grades!

They decided they were going to beat me up. So, I decided I wasn't going to let them. I didn't win. My dad was furious! He went to the houses of each of these guys and threatened to drag them and their fathers into the front yard. He may have actually done that, but he never told me. One thing was certain: those guys never bothered me again! Sadly, that same intensity and physical aggression would become misguided toward the things he loved most.

My parents divorced for various reasons. When my mother left my father, she took my sister and me when we were toddlers. The story told to me was that she was hiding with us from my dad and grandfather at a friend's house.

When my dad found out where we were, he and my grandfather showed up forcefully. The woman whose home we were in stopped my dad at the door. In response, he grabbed her by the throat and choked her until she passed out, leaving large bruises on her neck. He forcibly took me from that house and left.

Family Motto

Because of the leadership of my dad, our family didn't believe in being weak or laying down for anyone. My response in a particular instance was the same as my dad's would have been. An older guy shoved my much smaller brother, bouncing his head off the side of a bus. I exploded, letting this guy know what I was going to do to him. Wow, was I angry. He had the good sense to get away from me—quickly!

A little insight into our family motto: "Never be weak," was something we said and acted out while celebrating New Year's Eve every year. At the time we did it, it was serious, yet now, even thinking about it makes me laugh with embarrassment!

While we would all sit around our table, Dad would say, "We are Z's, and what do we do?" It was a frequent question, so we all knew how to answer. While holding glasses in a toast, we would yell, "WE KICK A**!" He would yell again, "What are we going to do this year?" With gusto, we would all reply, "KICK A**!" and clink our glasses together as he exclaimed, "That's right!" I still get messages during the New Year holiday from friends who think it is the funniest thing, simply saying, "What are we gonna do this year?"

On the other hand, on the days we were with my mom, she would bring us to a church that believed in the baptism of the Holy Spirit. Remember, the Spirit-filled church was the very topic we spent the other half of our time mocking! And this only amplified my dad's religion issues. For me, going back and forth between these two opposing views fostered a warped sense of what was right.

The times we were with dad after being at church, he would ask me, "Do you believe that crazy religion of your mother and her church?" To which I would promptly reply, "Absolutely not." He would say, "You better not, and I'm not kidding! If you want to participate in that, you can plan on staying there."

He would go on to address all of us, "If any of you ever choose any of that, and one day come begging me to be a part of your life and share in the success we have, I will say to you, 'I love you, but f*** you!'"

He was so violently serious about this that he would threaten any youth pastor or person who wanted to reach out to me regarding Christianity. He honestly believed that what he was doing was right. He was working in all the light he had. Consequently, I experienced a crippling fear that I might displease him when it came to the topic of God.

Hunger For God

During those days of going to church one day and denouncing everything about it the next, my spiritual hunger still grew. I started to recall my name being called over the wind, and my heart became warm toward God. Only, there was no way for me to make any real commitment, knowing I would shortly be grilled and pressured to verbally renounce everything about it. Regardless of the constant pressure to stay away from anything to do with God, I believe the Lord sent different people to pray for me.

One instance of this was through a kind, Scandinavian woman. She had a strong accent and came up to me at church one Sunday to ask when my birthday was. I told her, and she pledged to pray for me every day. She would also send me reminders on my birthday that she was praying for me. For many years, even after she moved back to Scandinavia, I received small gifts from her along with words of prayer and encouragement.

Additionally, when ministers would come to the church, they would often end up praying over me. Through all those moments, I was careful not to let my guard down, still knowing I would be giving a detailed account of the events to my dad in the next day or two.

Kidnapped

Everything took a significant turn, through rather unconventional means, during a hot summer week in August of 1990. My sister had been preparing for a volleyball tournament, and I had plans to be with friends until it was my dad's week again. However, my mom's parents came to visit us at her house, wanting to take all of us for a ride in their RV. My mom displayed an anxious willingness to get us in the RV, bringing some extra things along. It did seem strange to me at the time, but not enough to think twice about going along. I was thirteen years old, my sister twelve, and my brother nine.

After we had driven a few hours, they decided to stop and rest awhile. This turned into parking and staying for the night. This came as a surprise to us, so it was at this point the three of us were told that we weren't going back home, but continuing on in the morning to a family camp!

Grandpa, Grandma, and Mom had all conspired to kidnap us and take us to family camp. True story! Their purpose in being so secretive was to avoid my dad and grandfather finding out because they would protest and take legal action, given the occasion. My grandparents were wonderful people that sincerely loved the Lord and believed they had a word from God to get us to this camp and hear a particular speaker. Grandpa and Grandma were right in this action as far as it concerned me.

Their efforts that summer became the turning point into a series of events that set my life on a collision course with the living God. It still makes me laugh, thinking about my grandmother and grandfather—a mother of ten and a prayer warrior, and a successful businessman highly dedicated to the Lord—crafting this master plan together. Whatever the strategy was, they had heard God and obeyed, and I am forever grateful.

Supernatural Miracles

What awaited me at camp was an encounter that finalized my decision to follow Jesus. Little did I know, a wild man was ministering that week named Dave Duell.

Dave had a unique ministry filled with humor and amazing demonstrations of Holy Spirit power. He told captivating stories that were often hilarious, but it was his relationship with God that fascinated me most.

One of his many powerful stories was of the time he was invited to minister to Yasser Arafat and his staff. He also expounded upon the many times he had seen blind eyes open and deaf ears healed. He went on with volumes of testimonies about the supernatural things God had done for him. Honestly, up to that point, his message was the greatest thing I had ever heard.

When he finished speaking, he said, "Well, that's enough talking. It's time for some demonstration!" I thought, *Demonstration? He isn't going to try to do the stuff he talked about, is he? The stories were great, but surely that kind of thing won't happen here!*

Dave spoke again, "Does anyone here have asthma?" I looked around the room thinking, *Who would answer a question like that?* Suddenly, a person raised their hand.

"Get up here," Dave yelled. This person quickly came to the front, and my full attention was fastened on them. As soon as they got to the front, Dave said to them, "I'm going to chop that thing off!" He took his hand and, like an axe, ran it over their head and down their back, making a "Cha!" sound with the movement. My eyes widened as this person fell on the floor as though they had been shot dead! I gazed at them on the floor as Dave laughed in response to the asthma they "used to have!"

The place became electric over that person falling under the power of God. Before I knew it, many more people came forward and received the same touch of power. They were experiencing legitimate miraculous healing in their bodies! It was the most beautiful thing I had ever seen.

The thing that sealed the whole experience for me was when my 9-year-old brother went forward because he had a turned ankle that was causing him to have difficulty walking. It wasn't just a temporary condition, as he had been going to specialists to help him correct it.

Dave sat him down on the stage, my brother's legs dangling over the edge. Dave got down on one knee, picked up my brother's ankle and commanded it to be straight. To my shock, it straightened out—I watched it straighten out! Then his leg grew until it was even in length with the other.

Seeing this gave me the nerve to ask for prayer regarding a horrible allergy to bee stings that had caused me some awful experiences. Dave prayed for me, and the last thing I recall was coming back to my senses and looking at the ceiling because I had been knocked out by the power of God!

During one of those services, a person practicing witchcraft came to the front and screamed. Dave cast a demon out of her. When it came out, it sounded like something was roaring. It was that spirit shouting as it left the woman. It was scary, yet so powerful to see that woman free of the torment inside of her. She left the meeting that night entirely free!

A Cup Of Cold Water

This created a hunger in me for the Holy Spirit. At the end of that meeting, people in the parking lot needing prayer surrounded Dave. He prayed and kept ministering for hours! This made a great impression on me. So, I ran to the kitchen area and got a cup of water. I made my way through the compressed crowd and got in front of Dave and offered it to him. He took it with appreciation and drank it.

Then Dave asked me, "What do you want?" Without knowing where it came from or why I said it, I eagerly replied, "Boldness!" Dave responded with, "You got it!" He prayed over me and released the power of God for boldness into my life, and it still works today! When the Spirit of God comes on me to do something, that supernatural boldness rises.

One of the best parts about this meeting was that, not long after, I was stung by a bee on both my throat and face. Typically, it would have caused significant swelling and put me down for days. Yet, nothing happened!

After encountering Jesus and the Holy Spirit through the ministry of Dave Duell, my life changed. There was no going back. Everything I witnessed and received at this family camp was enough for me to go all-in and give my life to Jesus. I told God that whatever He had, I wanted it! Even if it cost me my life, there was now no other way I could live other than completely for Jesus.

Grandpa's Tragedy

One day, my mom came to me saying she had had a horrible dream about my dad's father. She had vividly seen him dead, so she had a strong impression to pray for him. It was obvious to me that this dream had truly shaken my mom because she kept talking about it.

One week later, I was sitting with her in the kitchen, my sister and brother nearby, when the phone rang. The voice on the other end caused her countenance to fall, and she broke into tears. My grandfather had been killed in a tragic farming accident. Even though I was grief-stricken, I still remembered that this was exactly what my mom had seen just a few days before.

The Ultimatum

It was also during this time that my newfound desire to serve Jesus became a point of contention with my dad. After those meetings, we went to visit him. He asked us about camp and what had happened.

He asked me, "Did you participate in what they did there?" This was routine, but this time my response was one of resolve and absolute faith in Jesus. I confidently answered, "Yes. I saw miracles and healings, but most importantly, my heart is wholly surrendered to Jesus."

There was no middle ground after saying this. The tension grew so thick, you could have cut it with a knife. His anger swelled and manifested. As he often would do when enraged, he took his shirt off and towered over me. He released an onslaught of intimidation and rage, mocking the miracles, accusing me of lying and laughed at me with a livid dismissal of any response I attempted.

Although I began with confidence, I ultimately broke into hysterical tears, and I knew it was all about to come to a head for him and me. He built up to his ultimatum. "You know where this goes! Did you think I was f****** joking?"

He knew I remembered the conversations we had regarding me inheriting our property and assets. He went on, "You better take a look at Duke and think about seeing him again."

He continued, "You need to think very carefully about what you're going to say to me when I ask you the question. Think about your brother and sister! You would be leaving them too! Your grandfather would be hurt and so angry with you! You know what I have said about all this!" Again, he was referring to me losing my inheritance.

20

"If that insanity is what you want, then f*** you, and go get it! But remember," he warned, "there is no coming back." He had said on numerous occasions, "If you ever leave me, one day, you will come back. When you realize all you could have had here, how good it was, you will find out how hard it is without me! It won't matter if you are starving or desperate. When you come back, the answer will still be the same: I love you, but f*** you! Now, get out."

It felt like my life was being shredded from the inside out. Nothing had prepared me for the intensity of a moment like this. We were both quiet except for my crying.

A few moments passed, and then he calmly made his offer. He said, "I will ask you one time tonight and you need to choose. In front of your family and God, I want you to choose. You can choose our family, or you can choose God."

Shaking and bawling, I gushed in pain, "Dad, I love you!" I went to hug him, but his arms stayed down at his sides. He remained quiet until I answered his ultimatum. I genuinely loved my dad; there were so many things about him that made him my hero. The same thought played through my mind on repeat, *This can't be happening!*

Finally, I answered through my tears.

"Jesus," I said. "My choice is Jesus." Immediately after saying this, emotions overwhelmed me, and I broke out sobbing, "It doesn't have to be one or the other!"

However, this was a non-negotiable decision for him. He said, "Okay, get your things." I had to get in the car and he drove me to my mom's house that very night.

I made many attempts to keep my dad in my life. I begged, "Let's be in each other's lives. Even if we can't agree on belief systems, let's at least be in contact." I reached out on many occasions in those early years, but the response was short and absolute, "You still doing that thing?"

"Yes," I would always reply.

"Then I haven't thought of you for one moment."

This choice resulted in walking through my teenage years without a relationship with my dad. Consequently, I relied instead on my growing relationship with my heavenly Father, the Living God of the Bible.

The Gorbachev Prophecy

Throughout the entire year after that experience with my dad, I developed a very close walk with the Lord which was amplified by a habit of devouring the Word of God. I would read entire books of the Bible in short periods of time. It became highly important to me that God's Word was inside of me. During that following summer, August of 1991, we went back to camp for a week to see Dave Duell again.

As the week had progressed, the meetings grew so large, they had to be taken outside due to lack of seating. As a result, chairs were set up in the parking lot and all the way up the opposing hill. Dave found himself preaching and ministering on the front steps of the building. It was thrilling for me to see people with such a hunger for God. I thought, *they are even willing to sit outside at night!*

A dramatic thing happened to me on one of the final nights. Dave said something that piqued my attention. A coup had risen in the now former Soviet Union , and their leader, Mikhail Gorbachev, was placed under house arrest.

In the context of these events with Gorbachev, Dave stood up under the power of the Holy Spirit and said, "I just heard the Holy Spirit say that this situation in Russia will be over shortly and Gorbachev will be set free."

It was a simple but unambiguous word from God. As I heard it, the power of the Holy Spirit overwhelmed me. It was the first time I had ever experienced a prophetic word that boldly predicted the outcome of a current event.

It was astonishing to me and my heart burned for more. History shows that it wasn't but a few days after the coup that the word Dave released came true and Gorbachev was free. This most recent encounter with the Voice of God woke something up inside of me. It was as if God said, "That's right, Joseph. I want to speak to you."

Flowing in the Spirit

During this season, after choosing to follow Jesus over family, I began to flow in the Spirit every chance I got!

The worship leader at this camp was a country western singer and guitarist by the name of John Peterson. He was a gifted musician and used to hang out with others, such as Waylon Jennings and Chet Atkins. This man sensed the call of God on my life and got permission from my mom to take me with him all over the United States as often as I could go.

His ministry was to youth, and we often ministered in boy's ranches, youth groups, churches, music festivals, and every place we could preach the gospel. He taught me how to play guitar and we would listen to worship and engage in Bible studies on the road. It was amazing. I met people on these trips who are still a part of my life today.

I remember praying over someone with John all those years ago, and as I put my hands on them a picture popped up inside me, and I said, "You have asthma, don't you? I can see it in your body!" Then I commanded it to come out, and the person was powerfully touched. John stared at me with wide eyes and said, "Wow!"

This was the beginning of a new season of supernatural encounters.

Chapter Three

A Supernatural Summer

At the age of fifteen, I was fatherless and wild. However, I devoured the Word of God and was willing to do anything God asked me to do. Submitting to authority was not something that was enjoyable to me. My thought was, *If I gave up my dad for God, then God is my authority.* So, it was a tender spot in my heart, and if someone pushed, I would come back at them, hard. Even though that type of dysfunction was working in me, there was still a deep desire for the things of God. So, if someone were a man of God, I would do anything for them without question, but I regarded anyone else as nothing.

During this time, John Peterson sought out getting me a summer position at the Christian camp where I had met Dave Duell two summers before. My mom and the leadership agreed to let me work the grounds, and in the kitchen, so that's exactly what I did.

After having grown up operating heavy equipment and tractors on our farm, mowing lawns was easy. Each night, services were held with guest speakers from around the world. During worship, I would intensely praise God.

My aggressive worship was filled with leaping into the air and dancing around with all my strength. It wasn't a joke to me. I figured if this was my path in life, then I was all in.

I met good friends that summer—friends I still have today. God's ultimate purpose for my being there was a setup. Who else knew that this season of my life was the foundation of my future calling?

Dr. Derstine

Dr. Gerald Derstine was the founder of this camp that had such an impact on my life. He was one of the fathers of the Charismatic movement and had ordained a number of well-known ministers, such as Benny Hinn, among others.

Dr. Derstine took special notice of me. He would have me help him mend fence lines and work with him on the lawns of the campus. The fact that a man of such notoriety would go out and work the way he would really spoke to me. He never expected anyone to do something he wasn't willing to do, and I respected him for that.

He and his wife, Beulah, saw something in me, so they had me travel with them throughout that summer. Sometimes we would drive many hours away to speak in various churches. This was a tremendous honor for me, especially because I was so young.

The van we traveled in was blue and had the name "Christian Retreat" on the outside. One time, we were driving swiftly through winding forest roads on our way to speak when a crow flew in front of us, violently striking the windshield precisely in front of Gerald's face. It ricocheted straight off the glass and high into the air, and I watched as it finally fell to the ground far behind us on the blacktop. This made an impression on me because Gerald had never even flinched! He trusted God and was focused intently on his mission.

When he preached, he always invited Beulah to join him on the stage to say hello. He would also ask me to the stage to talk to audiences about what God was doing in my young generation.

I told stories and shared encouraging thoughts, all the while feeling tremendously honored that I was given such a privilege. This brief time with them made a massive impact on me. I was honored to carry their bags, run their product table, and share the stage with them.

Thank you, Dr. Gerald Derstine.

White Stone

During this same summer, about halfway through the season, I was walking by the lake when I sensed the Holy Spirit speaking to me. I heard His Voice say, "Take off your shoes and wade out into the lake." I stopped for a moment and thought, *Did I just hear this right? Take off my shoes and walk out into that cold lake?*

After not hearing anything else, I thought to myself, *Okay, I'll do it*. Off came my shoes, and after rolling my jeans up as far as I could, I waded into the lake. The water was over knee deep when my feet stopped. Let me tell you, it was cold, and I felt odd.

Not knowing what else to do, I just stood there for a minute or two. Suddenly, I felt a gentle pull in my heart to turn to the right and walk a little more. Then the sense to stop brought me to a halt. Again, that same sense, as if speaking to me said, "Look down and pick up the first stone you find."

It was difficult to see into the water, but I did what I sensed I was supposed to do. Reaching down into that chilly water, I located a small stone. Standing upright with the stone in hand, I noticed that, unlike the other rocks in the area, the stone was white. I stood there for a moment and examined this marble-sized, white stone.

To my astonishment, it possessed natural grooves on its exterior, which were a very dark gray color. As I inspected the rock, it didn't take long to identify that these nearly black lines looked like letters, which spelled the word "Joe".

I had discovered a rock in the water onto which nature had carved *my name*! It was shocking, so I simply stood on the shore, my gaze fixed on this surreal, little, white stone. At that moment, I felt an overwhelming sense that the Lord had called me and is always with me.

Encounters

My primary purpose in sharing some of the stories in this chapter is to show that when you lay hold of the Word of God and realize your identity and authority in Jesus, it will bring order to any supernatural chaos in your life.

The latter half of that summer erupted with wild, supernatural encounters. That is the best way I can explain them: everything from wild, scary things, to confronting witches, to casting demons out of people.

The environment of the place we were in was known for supernatural encounters. Of course, this attracted many types of people from all over the world, people who had a hunger to have these supernatural experiences. During these meetings, people were consistently healed of sickness and set free from depression. It engaged a lot of individuals who dealt with dark spiritual issues as well.

Dealing with Witchcraft

There was one encounter that I will never forget. My friend Matt[1] and I were in a room to the side of the camp's main meeting place during a time when no services were happening. As we were inside praying, a lady walked in, praying strangely and loudly. It made the two of us feel very uncomfortable.

She approached us and said to me, "I'm going to lay hands on you." I immediately responded with a polite, "No, thank you."

However, she proceeded to lay hands on Matt, and he sat still as she spoke loudly over him in a creepy language. It was obviously not a Holy Spirit encounter at all! When she had finished, she burst into laughter and exited the room.

Matt looked at me and said, "I don't feel well." So I said, "Let's get you up to your place." As we walked, he said, "I felt something come over me while that lady spoke to me."

When we arrived at his house, Matt went to the restroom and became sick. Shortly after, his wife came out holding a baby. All of a sudden, chaos flooded the scene: the baby vomited on the floor and started screaming, the lights went out, and their stereo popped on, blaring loudly, without any logical reason for doing so.

I immediately ran to find help, but as I did, something came over me and I felt sick and angry, vomiting and falling

---

[1] This name has been changed to maintain confidentiality.

down on the sidewalk. People around me asked if I was okay, but I couldn't reply, due to both anger and sickness.

This next part sounds even more strange, but it is absolutely true. One young lady went into Matt's house to pray for his family, and when she walked through the door, she fell down and passed out. This wild experience continued until John Peterson went into the house and spoke the Word of God over it. Suddenly, it all stopped.

I was able to get off the sidewalk outside and find my way to a bed. Laying there, I felt hatred and anger to a degree I had never experienced before. Finally, I opened my mouth and said, "The victory is the Lord's, and I resist this, in Jesus' Name!"

Everything I was feeling—the anger, hatred, and sickness—left instantly! I got up as if nothing happened, other than feeling very dehydrated and weak.

Matt was rushed to the emergency room. I went to see him with John, another good friend, and my friend's dad. I will never forget that as we were walking along the street, a person shouted, "Jesus Christ!" from across the street while glaring at me. My friend's dad said, "Nope! Sorry, just one of His followers!"

We got to the hospital room where my friend was in bed receiving IV fluids. Matt said, "I had something come over me like darkness. I was terrified." We prayed for him, and he got better.

This impacted me greatly, and I decided I would never be a victim of something like that again. So, I began to read the Word of God even more than before. This put steel on the inside of me! I can remember thinking, *There is nothing like this Book!* The more I read it, the stronger and more secure I became.

Not long after this, the same lady was in the back of one of the meetings. There was a time of ministry when I was involved in praying over people. This lady came toward me, and I felt strength and authority rise up inside of me as she approached.

She was only a few steps from me, and she raised her hand as if to reach out and touch me. On the inside, I rose up and lunged at her in faith and power. I laid my hand on her and commanded whatever it was working through her to leave. She fell down like a dead person and just laid there.

I don't remember what happened after that, but I never saw that lady again.

Calling on Angels

Various people who struggled with demonic issues would come to the prayer room at the camp. I would pray for them, and demons would come out screaming. One young girl, who had been a part of occult practices, had a voice speak through her saying it would kill her and me. I was young and didn't know what to do, but there I was.

She wildly manifested demons and attacked me. Wow, she was strong! Her voice even changed. As she tried to harm both herself and me, I commanded the evil spirits to leave. However, this only made her behave more violently.

I read in the Word of God that angels obey the voice of the covenant—my voice. So, not knowing what else to do, I called on angels for assistance. Immediately, she was pinned to the floor like a starfish. It looked like someone had tackled her and thrown her to the floor in a Velcro suit! She was stuck to the floor and couldn't move. I said, "Thanks, angels!" It wasn't long before that girl was completely set free.

Another time, a young lady and I were riding in the backseat of a car moving fast down the highway. Along the way, she manifested a demonic voice and said, "I need air." After rolling down her window, she lunged out the opening and almost got all the way out!

Her hair was blowing hard in the wind, and I went out that window nearly as quickly as she had. I grabbed ahold of the back of her belt, but could not stop her hands from striking the ground at highway speed. It was awful. I was working hard not to let her arms and head hit the ground. It all happened so fast, but I was able to pull her back through the window. After arriving at our destination, we cast that destructive spirit out of her!

These types of experiences were routine throughout the second half of that summer of my fifteenth year.

An Insatiable Desire for the Word of God

These experiences made me ask the question, "What have I gotten into?" I didn't discover the turning point for dominating supernatural craziness until I realized that the key was the time I spent in the Word of God.

Through that season of supernatural encounters, I learned to develop an overwhelming hunger for the Word of God. It definitely took discipline at first. However, once I experienced its worth, it became the most valuable thing in my life.

The Word of God is how I learned to increase my sensitivity and master supernatural experiences. For me, it began with prayer, but the Word of God ultimately became the only thing that brought peace and order to supernatural bedlam.

I took it so seriously that spending time with the Word of God became a full-time occupation. This often meant reading—or listening—through the entire New Testament several times a week. This was like building my foundation with steel, rather than mere concrete or stone.

Hearing or seeing the unexplainable, or sensational experiences (what my five senses could detect), became secondary in importance to the Word. However, when it was time to exercise the gifting in my life, it came out with power! This greatly helped me, not only in this season, but also in every one that followed.

A Supernatural Knowing

One thing has always been present in my life, even from the time I was a young boy: a supernatural knowing. Like the *Rocky IV* story, sometimes I would say what I knew, but as time went on, it seemed better to me to keep those experiences to myself.

This knowing wasn't just regarding facts or events. Ever since those teen years, I had a heightened form of empathy that was nearly tormenting. This heightened sensitivity of what others were feeling could make it uncomfortable to even look people in the eyes because of what I would feel, which caused me to develop an introverted personality. My nature is to be very outgoing and social, so when I was around people who were close—friends or family—I didn't have the same sense of empathy, so I was extroverted. Close friends mostly knew me that way.

This sense of empathy was often magnified by looking at or being in close proximity to others. The sense of what they felt was not necessarily an emotional, moment-to-moment tracking of their every feeling, but rather a revelation of a deeper, more permanent part of their identity.

A knowing would rise up inside of me that conveyed whether a person was sweet, depressed, angry, perverted, or something else. For example, if a person was not to be trusted, I would experience a sense of distrust or a feeling that the person was working an angle or being manipulative.

There were other times I would sense the good in people whose displayed bad behaviors. In those cases, when I saw their obvious potential, I'd overlook the bad and only act according to the good I sensed in them.

Friends have asked me (regarding different people), "Don't you know who this person is, or what they are like?" There hasn't always been a good answer because my sense about the true nature of a certain person might override the obvious negatives. Even when these individuals behave negatively toward me, my response is most often like water off a duck's back.

Why? Because deep inside of certain people resides potential and good that is trying to get out. I discovered that if I stay in my anointing, show mercy, and call to the good in those individuals—based on that sense of empathy—they have a real chance at winning! The Lord has brought many people into my path for this purpose. Through the simple belief—of even just one person—of the good in them, He has brought them to a higher realization of their identity in Jesus.

There has been another side to this empathy. Sometimes the people who are the most adored and loved by many are the ones for whom I carry a sense of repulsion. **False humility is a hard thing for me to be around.** If someone is a little arrogant, or even rude, but remains true to their inner self, although they may not pleasant, at least they are being authentic.

However, false humility, or a spirit of competition, is very repulsive to me. There has never been a formula to this, but most often when this sense arises, I have learned to trust that sense over the face value of an individual.

These supernatural encounters, and my empathic sensitivity, were part of a bigger picture that needed to be refined in my life. The Word of God and the Holy Spirit are the best teachers! However, I discovered that there are avenues of development that can move you into your lane even faster.

Chapter Four

Graveyard Encounter

I came into contact with two voices which tried to speak to me at a young age. One was the Voice of God, and the other brought fear and uncertainty. I discovered that this was the voice of darkness that took the form of a spirit that was allowed to operate on both the family property and in the members of my family. That spirit working in and around my family was somewhat of a regular occurrence, and always terrifying. However, at the age of sixteen, I put a stop to that fearful voice."

I was home, following the summer of the supernatural experiences I wrote about in the previous chapter, and began to seek God. I had been leading people to the knowledge of Jesus at my school, even praying over people who received healing. One night, while I was praying, I took a significant turn.

Being prompted by the Holy Spirit at around midnight, I felt the urge to go to my paternal grandfather's grave. I felt little hesitation in my heart, even though it was a peculiar thing to be prompted to do. However, I recognized it as the same prompting which led to my discovery of the white stone. That had turned out pretty well, so I obeyed!

The sense I had was that the Holy Spirit was instructing me to go to the cemetery to cut off every curse over my life so that it could no longer influence me or affect my future family. I was to draw a line by making a declaration which would stop the progress of any evil thing that had ever happened in my family history.

My heart thought, *Who am I to disagree with this prompting?!* So, I responded, "Yes, Sir," got into the car, and pulled into the country cemetery within a half hour, arriving somewhere between twelve-thirty and one o'clock in the morning.

It was completely dark. There was no light, except the soft light of the moon filtering through the trees. Usually the black-as-ink darkness would have terrified me, especially in a creepy cemetery. But this particular night, the Spirit of God came upon me with peace and authority.

Without hesitation, I shut off the headlights of my car and confidently made my way to my grandfather's grave, weaving in and out among the tombstones, with only that faint light of the moon to guide me.

Finally, I stood in front of my grandfather's headstone. Poised in silence for a few minutes, a boldness for my legacy and future family rose up inside me, accompanied by a righteous and indignant anger. Rather than fear—being in an eerie graveyard barely one lumen above pitch black—I felt an attitude of aggression against the things that had held my lineage bound.

I passionately declared that every curse was broken: "As for me and my house, we will serve the Lord! And in the

Name of Jesus, no physical or spiritual curse will follow me from this day forward!" I boldly drew a line in the spirit realm. I made many such declarations for what seemed like a half-hour, first to the Lord, then to the kingdom of darkness, as I informed it that this was now my legacy and that Jesus would be glorified through my family after me.

I did this with a heart of love and respect for everyone before me who had simply lived in the light they had. However, it was imperative that I cut off anything and everything that was ungodly from the past behavior of any of those from whom I was descended. I rejected abuse, sexual wickedness, addiction, witchcraft, violence, etc.

This was the point in my life where all the negative spiritual "traffic" instantly ceased. The tormenting things I had heard as a boy were permanently silenced. From that moment forward, the only voice I developed a sensitivity to hearing was the voice of the Holy Spirit. Other things attempted to knock on my door, but Jesus and the Word of God answered.

About a week after the cemetery experience, I walked into a youth meeting, held at the church I attended. This particular evening I came in late, and when I walked in the door, a young lady saw me and instantly manifested demons. She went into convulsions and fell to the floor. *Whoa*, I thought, *what is happening?* Yet, it was obvious to me that it was full-tilt demonic.

Now, it's important to understand that this was a "seeker-friendly" church. The culture was, "Let's play music, play games, and maybe do a drama or puppet show to reach people for Jesus."

A demonic manifestation was not the norm and was a radically new experience for this crowd. The young people responded by crying and panicking, not knowing at all what to do when a demon manifested. Some of the kids ran away while others encircled the girl, trying to calm her down. It was chaos!

Yet, the Spirit of the Lord came upon me with an overwhelming sense of peace. I walked over to her and calmly said, "You come out of her, in Jesus' Name." She replied, "The voices saw you; they told me not to talk to you!"

"Okay, I don't care about the voices," I replied. "They can go now, in Jesus' Name." With all the demonic theatrics you can imagine, she told me the names of two entities that were speaking through her.

"I couldn't care less what their names are," I said. "Now, leave!"

In one final attempt to stay, these demonic voices piped up through the young lady with gnarly voices, saying, "We saw you in the graveyard—we were there! We know you, and we know what you were doing!" They laughed and mocked me.

This really got my attention! A holy anger came upon me, and I snapped back, "Who cares where you were and what you've seen?! Now, get out of her, and leave this place!"

The girl sat up and turned her attention to my friend, who was not in the Word, but like so many of the others, had just come for a "seeker-friendly" meeting.

With a mocking demeanor, she said, "He doesn't believe, he is afraid." So, I sent him out of the room. Then I said, "I believe in Jesus, and you are beaten. Now, get out of here, and I don't want to hear another word from you." In that instant, the girl went limp, fell back to the ground, and the two demons left.

After she had recovered, she explained to me that she was a young witch who was part of a coven that came to disrupt the service. After our encounter, she abruptly left.

I thought it was thrilling that the kingdom of darkness had been impacted by what the Spirit of God led me to do a week earlier. It was confirmation to me that my offensive attack against the darkness in my family had worked!

Bonfire

Not long after experiencing this demonic manifestation at the church, my mom hosted a church bonfire at her house. At these bonfire parties, we would set an enormous stack of wood and brush on fire. Everyone would drink hot cider, hang out together, play football, and simply enjoy one another's company.

As I was walking around at the party, I came to the front of the house and saw that same girl standing there. However, this time she was not alone. A man in a long black coat stood with her.

He stared at me for a while, until I said, "May I help you guys?" I don't even know how they found my place or even knew about the bonfire. I assumed it was through asking around where I lived, but no one in my circle knew who these two people were.

She gestured to the man next to her and said, "This is my warlock."

I simply replied, "Hello, warlock. You guys want some apple cider or something?" He remained silent, so I said, "I'm gonna head over by the fire again. Have fun!" I had been in the Word and broken so much stuff off my life that this was a non-issue to me.

I continued to walk and mingle at the party a bit, then I went back into the house. When I walked in, I found the two of them inside. He wanted to speak to me about power.

I said, "Yeah, you want to know about that? What would you like me to teach you?"

He said, "I can curse people."

"Great!" I replied. "Because Jesus in me breaks every curse." I literally treated him as though the topic of conversation was boring. This was the first time I understood that **the kingdom of darkness is nothing unless you allow it to be something**. I could tell that my complete lack of concern annoyed him.

I was leaning against the kitchen counter at this point and just started telling him jokes. Don't ask me why, it just seemed appropriate. He couldn't believe I was telling jokes! They both stepped away from me, so I walked back outside to the party and talked to a few people.

Time passed, and I went back into the house again. They followed me into the kitchen and I noticed they were both bleeding down their arms.

"What happened?" I asked them. "Did you fall down or something?" Then I realized they were cutting themselves to get pretty good blood flow. They began to lick and drink it the best they could.

"Gross!" I really don't know if this was the right thing to say or not. Remember, this girl already had demons come out of her at the church, and instead of staying to get help, she had bolted and returned to her nasty setting.

I got angry, grabbed the warlock by the shoulder, and threw him out the front door. As they were both standing in the front driveway, I said, "If you came here for help, I'm your guy. If you came here to continue this kind of stuff, and want to continue, then I'm gonna knock you out."

I gave him an ultimatum to either knock off that behavior or get knocked to the ground. They were trying to curse me, so I told them, "Your curses have no power and are laughable. What kind of person tries to obey their spiritual force by drinking blood? Only a total loser would do that. You and the devil are total losers. If you want a life, I have it for you. But if you're going to push the issue, I will smack you right in the mouth and throw you out of here." They abruptly turned and left. I never saw them again.

Now, I'm not saying I handled the situation exactly right. Please remember, I was only 16! However, I was learning how to walk in boldness and to deny the kingdom of darkness influence over my life in any way.

The Discovery of Authority

It is a profound thing to me that there is such significance in cutting off spiritual things. What I did at the graveyard shook the kingdom of darkness enough to send agents to my church and home to confront me!

I learned that my authority in Jesus is based on what He did. However, it is my enforcement of what He did that releases His power in this world. I realized that not only had I stopped the negative encounters from when I was much younger, but even more importantly, knowing Jesus through His Word gave me authority over anything that might stand in front of me.

Walking in the authority of the Name of Jesus became my way of life. Many people are unwilling to "give up to go up". What I mean is that they are not willing to follow Jesus, no matter the cost. When you truly surrender all to Him you enter into a position of absolute authority.

In Matthew 16:24-25, Jesus said, *"If anyone desires to come after Me, let him deny himself, and take up his cross, and follow Me. For whoever desires to save his life will lose it, but whoever loses his life for My sake will find it."*

This is what giving up to go up means: if you lose your life by exchanging it for the life of Jesus, you will actually gain everything you never knew you wanted! There is a higher way to live, and it is found in the truth of the Gospel. When you discover it, it will make you bold!

Chapter Five

Encountering Prophets

Let's go back to those meetings with Dave Duell. At one point, he mentioned his nephew who had asked God if he could meet a prophet. This inspired me, making something on the inside of me jump. I did not possess the proper understanding of what an actual prophet was, so the term intrigued me. So, one day I said to the Lord, "If there are any real prophets today, I want to meet one."

Over the course of those early years, I met various people who claimed to be prophets. While I was attending a youth conference in Minneapolis, one particular event of interest occurred. The keynote speaker was a man named John Paul Jackson. He was known as a prophet who knew the Voice of God. He was also a seer: someone who could see things about people's current lives or potential future events.

During this conference, speakers talked, one session after another, with times of prayer as well. It wasn't until I heard John Paul speak and minister that something significant happened. He was different than the others, and what I felt when he shared was different as well.

He shared a message in the same format as the other speakers, but following his message, he did something none of the others did. At the close of his message, he took a moment, became still, and slowly surveyed the audience. He looked around the room up into the stadium seating, panning his eyes left and right as if looking for something.

This went on for a brief time, until he rested his eyes on an individual and calmly pointed them out. He told them things he was seeing about them, and then moved on to another person. He continued in this fashion for several minutes.

The arrangement of the meeting space was stadium style seating, as there were several hundred people in attendance. The audience ascended upward with each subsequent row from the stage. He continued pointing out different people in this sizable audience, telling them things no one could know about their lives in clear detail.

As this was happening, Dave Duell's prediction about Mikhail Gorbachev came to mind. John Paul's ministry to the crowd felt the same: it was thrilling to experience so many people being impacted in such a unique way.

Suddenly, to my surprise, John Paul looked at me. My heart pounded as he paused, gazing at me as if he was looking through me. His eyes were steely, which made me think, *Please don't say anything to me!* My seat was located on the front row of this packed out college gymnasium, one of the best places to see from any angle, so there was nowhere to hide.

I was wearing a cross around my neck made of twisted metal—a gift from my mother. It had distinct metallic colors, mostly charcoal, bright with worn silver on its high points. He identified me by referring to this unique item.

I gulped hard when he pointed at me, "Young man wearing the iron cross..." John Paul went on to describe many things about me, my future, and declared that I had a mighty calling. He also went into great detail about a woman that God had set apart for me. He even went into detail about her life: how she was and the current challenges she was experiencing. He said that she would come through those things and was being prepared for me.

Man, did I feel put on the spot! He charged me by saying I was to bring protection over her life and that God would use me as a covering that would save her life. There were many more details he shared, all of which impacted me greatly.

After the service, I was invited to speak with him. I can vividly recall his strong eyes. I was surprised when standing with him that he was a lot taller than me. He was happy to speak with me about what he had told me, and helped me understand anything I had questions about. I was thankful for the opportunity to speak with him.

This moment made me think, *Wow, God answered me: I finally met a prophet!* Little did I know, this moment was only a small fraction of God's answer to my prayer. It seemed that every time I met someone prophetic, they would prophesy many powerful things over me. They nearly always revolved around two recurring themes: my future wife, and my future wealth. He was preparing me for a future day when He would place excessive amounts of resources into my hands, to manage and distribute wealth.

A Busy Season

At the age of 18, my home church hired me to run their youth program. It was funny because as I was out to eat with the pastor one day, he asked me, "How old are you, anyway?"

"Eighteen," I replied.

"You're only eighteen?" he laughed. "Wow, we thought you were in your twenties! Let's not broadcast your age to everyone, okay?" he politely added.

I agreed, as I had already been on staff for a while. They must have thought I was older due to my responsibilities at the time. I was running youth camps, as well as music events, and frequently traveled across the country. I was teaching the Word while helping at church and events wherever I could.

We had hundreds of young people coming to these week-long events which had impressed my church. The youth group I pastored was well known for being a very alive ministry to young people. These summer youth programs I was overseeing were several hours away from my home church and I was simultaneously pastoring the youth program there as well.

This created a very busy season in my life, especially in the summertime. In the off-season, I worked several jobs, including all-night shifts, construction work, cleaning houses and carpets, grocery stores, car washing, and anything else I could do to make ends meet.

A Defining Encounter

A defining encounter occurred on my twentieth birthday. It was a Sunday morning, and my pastor was hosting a guest speaker. This particular meeting was in a school gymnasium that our church was renting at the time.

This guest speaker also happened to be a prophet. I thought, *Well, I've seen some of this ministry before.* However, there was such a stirring inside of me before he got up to minister, and I wasn't sure why it was happening, but the presence and power of the Holy Spirit was nearly palpable. There was a deep sense of something powerful and significant, as though God was going to appear or something. I hadn't felt this type of sensation since I first saw Dave Duell.

After the pastor introduced the guest minister, he walked to the front of the meeting and began to speak. I don't remember what his message topic was, but I will never forget the ministry time.

After a lengthy message, he stopped preaching and stood directly in front of me like a general. As he did so, the Word of the Lord came to him, and he boldly spoke words over me.

He told me about the call of God on my life and how I would reach many lives around the world. He said that when my time was done, those I discipled would do even more than I had, on a global scale. At one point, he talked about my future wife and how the Lord had preserved her for me (again, that word came).

He ministered over me with such accuracy and clarity that I was floored and in awe of the Holy Spirit. I will never forget the main point he drove home to me: "The Lord is requiring you to step into a long season of much learning. You need much training, much learning, much being teachable! You have the heart, but you must acquire knowledge."

It was so good for me to hear that. Those words lit a fire in me to learn and become better equipped. There were many more powerful words that were spoken by that man to me. I felt the significance of the Holy Spirit's calling over me burning deep.

45 Minutes of Fire Alarms

As he finished saying these things, and so much more, I sensed the Holy Spirit say, "Happy Birthday." No sooner had this come through my heart than the prophet stepped into a middle aisle and ministered to a woman halfway back in the meeting. As he told her that God wanted to touch her life, she jumped to her feet and screamed. She shouted in a grisly voice, "I will kill this woman before I ever let her free! She is mine! You cannot have her—I will kill you!" At exactly that moment, the fire alarms in the gymnasium sounded.

The demon inside this woman screamed threats through her as the fire alarms blared. The prophet's response was great.

He assured the crowd, "Nobody worry; this is normal."

Normal?! I thought. *How could this be normal?* Yet, whereas a jarring sense of panic had been present in the beginning, now—in the midst of sirens and alarms shrieking, a few ambulances and fire trucks in full alert, and a screaming demon—there was an unexplainable peace that flooded the gym.

It is a miracle we could still hear the speaker through the sound system. He took authority of the demon and told the woman to sit down. She did, and remained quiet.

However, the alarms didn't stop! They continued for 45 minutes. During the entire time, no one moved, and the prophet went throughout the room, with authority and power, sharing astonishing details with many people.

When the alarms finally stopped, he just continued ministering. No one left for hours. In fact, what started as a typical Sunday morning ministry went into the night and carried on into several weeks of meetings.

50

Here is an interesting side note about that Sunday meeting: We later discovered that there was a couple who decided to try something different for church this particular Sunday. They said to one another, "Let's try one of those charismatic churches." So they looked up our church in the directory and came that morning for the first time. Wouldn't you know, they chose seats directly in front of the woman who stood up with a demon speaking through her!

When this happened, the woman was leaning over this couple, grabbing the back of their chairs while screaming. They had never been to a Spirit-filled service before! It makes me laugh a little, imagining what their conversation might have been like on the way home. They must have thought all charismatic meetings are like that all the time!

That Sunday turned into about three years of doing periodic weeks of meetings that would often last all night, and drew large crowds. The mayor of the city attended, and the whole occasion made the newspapers. Many thrilling and amazing things happened during this season.

My life became engaged with the Voice of God in a way that I had never known. After being exposed to this type of setting, the gifting in my life was stirred and became more active than ever before. My dreams became prevalent and filled with details of events, people, places and scenery that I had never seen in person. These dreams always came a day or two before walking into that exact place, meeting those exact people. It was a wild ride!

The encounters with this prophetic ministry greatly impacted my life. One word that was given to me was in a private leadership meeting. I was pulled aside by the prophet and he declared over my future. Calmly and with authority, he told me that the Lord called me to a higher walk of purity. If I kept myself pure and waited, I would receive the absolute best, like a fine prime rib. He closed the word he was speaking over me by saying, "As you wait, it will be a sign to you at 7 o'clock in the evening. It will be raining on that day. You will know that God has been with you every step of the way."

The leadership chuckled a little as the word was given. As colorful as that statement sounded, It was very powerful to me, and I took it very seriously. It had always been highly important to me that I waited for my wife, but this word from the man of God really caused me to walk the line!

My First Open Vision

There was a season in the mid-1990s when, all over the world, there were meetings where the power of God was on display. These meetings drew unusually large crowds, which made them stand out. Two of the most well-known were in Toronto, Canada and Brownsville, Florida.

Shortly after the meeting on my birthday, I was invited to go to the Brownsville Revival. It took over thirty hours by bus to get from Duluth, Minnesota to Florida—that was a miserable ride.

When we arrived at our destination, the line of people camping out to get into the meetings was quite a sight! It seemed to be nearly a half-mile long. Everyone was outside in lawn chairs, talking with one another about where they were from and what Jesus had done for them. People from all over the world were there; it was amazing!

We got into the meeting shortly before the service began, and the presence of God in that place was powerful. Many people were getting healed, delivered, and saved. We went to those meetings for days.

On the final day, after being in that environment, rich in faith and power, we boarded the bus home.

As I was sitting on the bus, waiting for everyone else to get all their luggage on board, I suddenly found myself in a dreamlike state. I wasn't sleeping, but neither was I awake. I was still aware of my surroundings, but there was also another picture opening in front of me. It was as if I was opening a second set of eyes.

It was fully dimensional; more real than a movie or video. I saw a long piece of ground, with shrubs and trees off to each side. As this living picture unfolded, the ground became even more noticeable. It was hardened, and as the image became clearer, it was revealed to not be ground at all, but concrete.

Everything under my feet, and in every direction, was actually thick, solid concrete. While looking around, I noticed my hand. In it was a small seed. This seed was lighter in color and half the size of a sunflower seed. I watched myself interact with the seed, pinching it between my thumb and index finger.

After surveying the area once more (now with the seed between my fingers), I poised myself into a stance as if I were an Olympic athlete preparing to launch a javelin. When the prompting arose, I stepped forward and lobbed the seed into the air, upward and away from me, hard enough that my right foot came off the ground, like a baseball player throwing a ball high and far. It seemed almost gentle at first, gliding up into the air away from me, but when gravity took over and the seed finally came down, it hit the ground with such force that I jumped back in shock!

The little seed violently slammed into the concrete like a two-ton wrecking ball had been dropped from three hundred feet. Its impact produced a violent explosion, producing a barbaric crunching sound, like a meteor strike. As the seed punched through that thick concrete, the ground bounced into broken pieces as it sought the soil beneath.

The violent breakthrough revealed a large crater with broken concrete slabs standing on end and sideways, the way broken ice would sit if something broke the surface of a frozen lake. Only, these concrete remnants were lying in broken pieces inside the slope of this crater, which had a diameter of at least twenty feet.

I stared in wonder at this intense sight until the Voice of God suddenly spoke to me, "So shall your words be."

Suddenly, I was completely aware of my surroundings on the bus, not knowing what to say to those around me. That was the first time God had spoken to me so clearly, with such intensity.

The impact of this open vision was potent. After arriving back home from that long trip there was a newfound fire in me to tell everyone about the Good News of Jesus. When we have a genuine encounter with the Holy Spirit, it is for a purpose. Mine was to become a voice of the Gospel. More than ever before, I had a boldness and Holy Spirit determination to speak liberty to the hearts and souls of everyone I met.

God is looking for anyone who will simply let go and completely sell out to Him. Through this surrender, He will do amazing things and take you to places beyond your wildest dreams. He desires for each one of us to become a voice for Him.

Chapter Six

I Will Go

Leading up to the encounter with the prophet at church on my birthday, I had been in a relationship with a girl who I had in mind to eventually marry.

One particular day, the Holy Spirit came to me and told me that it was time for me to get out of this relationship. I asked Him, "Lord, have I done something wrong?" There wasn't a sense of wrongdoing, just an urgency to follow His leading. I really liked this girl, but I knew when the Lord was speaking to me.

The next time we were in each other's company, I brought the topic up and said what I needed to do. It was not a fun conversation, as she had been making plans to be married as well, but she understood.

This was not a simple season. I questioned the Lord and honestly just wanted to continue the relationship. Yet, there was no peace present to do so. It has become a vital rule in my journey to never violate that peace, even with good intentions.

It was April. A prophet came to hold a series of meetings, along with his wife and daughter. The first time I saw this girl, I blushed because of how pretty she was. Seriously, it was embarrassing. But I feared God and the prophet!

At this particular time, we were hosting a weekend day session, and his daughter was sitting in. At lunchtime, the pastors, along with the prophet and his wife, all left together for some ministry business. His daughter would be left behind, so her mom was attempting to arrange a ride for her from the church. Since I was present when they were trying to find her a ride, her mom elected me!

Thrilled (yet, terrified at the same time), I introduced myself. "Hello, my name is Joe."

"My name is Heather," she replied. "Looks like I'm stuck here, unless you're my ride?"

"Yes, I am," I said awkwardly. "Wanna go?"

"Sure," she said.

At the time, my cousin was with me for a ride as well, so the three of us made our way to my van. Now, this was not just any van! It was a maroon, wood-sided minivan from the mid-1990's. I had scraped together everything I could to get it, but it was definitely not a fashion statement that would impress a good-looking, cultured, city girl like Heather. Nonetheless, it was my ride, so she got into the van, and we set off to find something to eat.

I was so nervous, I offered her a pair of sunglasses that I had laying around. She politely said, "Umm, no, thanks," with a beautiful smirk on her face. As we were driving around, I got her laughing, which was a huge attention grabber for me. I thought to myself, Good job; she's laughing!

All of a sudden, her laughter transformed into screaming. Really screaming! In the key of, "Oh my God, I don't want to die right now!"

I whipped my head straight ahead, eyes back on the road, realizing I had turned onto a major highway, *the wrong way*, into oncoming traffic! Car after car hurtled straight for us at high speed! I swerved back and forth several times to miss cars coming up the steep hill. Finally, I swung aggressively to the left, tires squealing, and made it onto a street off the highway.

Heather was still yelling. Then, nervously, with wide eyes, began to laugh. She exclaimed, "That was the most hilarious thing ever!"

That got my attention. The typical girls I had been around would have flipped out. Right then, I knew that Heather was special.

Now that we were again safely driving down the street, my cousin, seated in the middle back seat, stared at me with deadpan eyes though the rearview mirror. He silently mouthed, "Moron," while discreetly pointing at me. I kept smiling (while listening to Heather talk) and laughing about the experience, while simultaneously staring back at him with eyes that said, "Shut up, or I will kill you."

From that day forward, Heather and I became inseparable. She lived in Minneapolis but would often travel to Duluth to attend our church. Eventually, this led to her moving to Duluth.

At the time, she had been pursued by a few guys, all claiming to be in love with her. In the humor of the Lord, her apartment phone number was identical to the pastor's home number, with the exception of two numbers being reversed. I will never forget the time one of these guys called for her.

One day, the phone rang while I was at the pastor's house. Being the only one home, I picked it up. To my surprise, it was a guy who was pursuing Heather. He thought he had called her apartment. I was thrilled to explain that he had called me instead! He fumbled all over himself, trying to explain how he would never want to steal someone's girlfriend and that he wasn't that type of guy.

I agreed, "Of course you're not because that would make you a loser. Only an untrustworthy weasel would do that. I'm so glad you are not like that or we would have a real issue. Thanks for calling me to let me know you're a man of honor."

I ended it with, "Have a great day. I will let Heather know you called," then abruptly hung up on him.

Prior to meeting me, Heather was going through the paces to join the Marine Corps, but decided against it at the last moment. Additionally, she was studying to be a surgical tech. However, the Lord had different plans for both of us.

A Supernatural Ring

During the early part of this season it was becoming more and more clear that Heather was going to be my wife, and she knew it as well.

Time was often a rare commodity between family, camp and church. These activities were all consuming at times. Yet, for Heather, there came a time during her decision-making process when she wanted to be in my vicinity regardless of the circumstances. I felt the same way about her. We were willing to change plans, drop jobs, and work to be in the same location as often as we could.

One summer, Heather took a position as the children's minister at the camp where I worked. (She has always been amazing with kids!) This gave us the ability to spend our free time together.

It wasn't long before I went to her father and asked for his permission to marry her. The answer was yes. The only issue was that I didn't have money to buy a ring. So, after borrowing money from a friend, I purchased a very simple engagement ring.

Heather and I were out for a walk one day and ended up on a dock that stretched out onto a nearby lake, part of a small park. I got down on my knee and held out the ring. Heather started crying. She didn't even say, "Yes," because she was so happy!

As we embraced on the dock, it began to rain, so we decided we should get going. I was amazed when we noticed the time: 7 o'clock in the evening.

I remembered the word that had previously been spoken over me regarding waiting and remaining pure for marriage: *"As you wait, it will be a sign to you at 7 o'clock in the evening. It will be raining on that day. You will know that God has been with you every step of the way."* The word had been upheld and the sign had happened. God had been with me every step of the way!

Heather knew there was no way for me to afford a wedding ring for her. So, we agreed it would be okay and we would do that down the road after we were married. This was hard for me to accept but necessary in the circumstances.

That is, until a divine appointment occurred during one of the evening services at the family camp. At the end of a service, a woman came over to me and told me a story of a lost marriage and how the Lord had spoken to her about something. This woman didn't know me, and I didn't know her, but she continued, staring at me intensely.

She said, "I must tell you something. The Lord guided me to do something some time ago." She really focused in on me at this point and went on to say, "The Holy Spirit told me to charge you with a promise that you must make, right now."

I said, "I'm not sure how to respond to that statement."

She nearly cut me off, asking, "You are going to be married? Is this true?"

"Yes," I replied.

She said, "I charge you before the Lord that you will care for her and protect her for the rest of your life."

Being a reasonable and honorable request (albeit from a complete stranger), I answered, "I can make that promise."

The woman continued, "I was instructed to purchase a never worn wedding ring and bring it to the person the Holy Spirit showed me." She then revealed in her hand a beautiful and valuable diamond ring. It was the exact style and cut Heather had pointed out to me weeks earlier! "This is yours to give her, if you promise to hold fast to my request."

My eyes began to cloud with tears as I agreed. She handed me the ring, hugged me, and that was the last time I saw her.

Later that night, I pulled Heather into the door of my cabin saying, "I have something to show you." I revealed the ring, "We get to be married properly and with a ring worthy of you." I put it on her finger and it fit! We both cried and thanked the Lord for His faithfulness and kindness to us.

We were so thrilled to tell everyone about it. At one point, we happened to be in the same area where my dad lived, and Heather said she wanted to meet him. You can imagine the interesting thoughts that went through my mind. However, it seemed right that she at least meet him. So, I decided to call him.

When he found out that Heather was with me, he said, "Come over." This led me to believe there was a chance of having some form of relationship with him. He was courteous to her but attempted to make me look like a fool. He basically wanted her to know what a great guy he was and how off I was regarding my life choices. It was a highly insulting and hurtful moment. Instead of anger, all I could do was cry from deep disappointment.

We politely said our goodbyes and never went back. There were no regrets over the moment because it was good for Heather to meet him.

Our Wedding Day

Heather and I had an awesome wedding! My friends gathered into a band and played the music, even an original song I wrote for her. It was a very memorable celebration for many people—especially the two who got married that day!

Seeing Heather walk down the aisle toward me was such a tremendous moment.

My pastor's message that day was so powerful for us. He said the Lord spoke to him a unique message that he had never done at any wedding before. He gave a message about Jonathan and his armor-bearer. Jonathan said, "I purpose to go over that river and see the Philistine outpost." The armor-bearer replied, "I will go."

He taught about how Jonathan went out against his father's wishes, which was especially meaningful to me. As he gave the teaching, my pastor looked at me as if to say,

"You have done well." He went on to describe the teamwork of Jonathan and his armor-bearer as a parallel to how the Lord would lead Heather and me all the days of our lives. He quoted Joshua saying, "No one will be able to stand up against you all the days of your life."

The words of my mentor and teacher sank deep into my being. It was like the Lord Himself was saying these words to me. With a profound sense of fulfillment and completion, I knew I was marrying the right one.

There was also the overwhelming impartation of responsibility to fulfill the calling of God on our lives, as I felt Him drawing us to a strong assignment we had yet to discover. Heather was the largest blessing God could have ever given me; He definitely knew what He was doing when He put us together. Thank You, Jesus, for Your graciousness!

Chapter Seven

You Cannot Live on
Another Man's Revelation

Abuse or domination over a person is never the will of God. However, it comes easiest in the area of religion, where it can be most destructive. Why? Because people are always looking for someone to follow, yet in the face of the heart of people to please God, the wrong leader may step in to declare, "Here is how!"

This has damaged innumerable lives over the course of history. For many who have walked out of damaging religious experiences, some of the things I will share in this chapter will be nothing new. However, the desire is that in the telling, some of you will find reprieve, hope and the courage to break free.

Perhaps you have left an abusive scenario and have lost the ability to trust. Through this chapter, may you find healing. For those who have not endured these types of circumstances, may you have a better understanding and compassion for those who have.

The Beginning of an Extreme Season

It was an extreme time, mixed with both tremendous opportunities and intense challenges. Newly married, and willing to do the highest calling God had for us, Heather and I were seeking where we should be and what we should do.

I was still responsible for a number of events, as well as leading at a large capacity for our age. The church we were attending took a hard hit due to a serious moral fall of the pastor. We stuck around to love and attempt to restore this godly man, with whom I had cut my teeth on biblical studies. It was very difficult to see the place that should have been our church home fall to shambles and become leaderless.

For that season, it seemed best to find work and I was soon hired on at a cutting-edge aircraft factory. The job was a wonderful experience, sometimes giving me the opportunity to go to airshows with the company pilots to show off our company's various aircraft.

We were also being invited to minister at various places on weekends by people familiar with us from the conferences and meetings from years prior. Yet, life wasn't fulfilling during this time. It felt like driving with the parking brake on. There was always a burning desire to do something for the Lord without splitting time at a job. It was in the middle of that time that we were blessed and thrilled by the introduction of our first baby.

Everything took a turn when I met a very gifted leader in the area of the prophetic. It was an answer to what I was looking for. The organization Mr. Leader[2] led reached leaders around the world in a variety of realms such as politics and international business. The impact he had was remarkable!

---

[2] This name has been changed to maintain confidentiality.

Mr. Leader was literally impacting global leaders through private meetings where the Lord would speak through him to change the lives of these very influential people. This was so impressive to me, especially after witnessing the might of these encounters several times in person. This brought about the decision to dedicate all our time and energy to his vision.

This was the answer! There was an opportunity to serve at this organization, and it was thrilling to have him interested in what I could offer! With great enthusiasm, we made a major commitment to work for this highly impactful leader.

This led to a strictly dedicated sixteen years of day and night availability. The beginning years were truly a privilege and the training received was world-class. Much of what we learned from his leadership is still implemented in much of our ministry functions today.

The largest lesson of that sixteen-year journey is the invaluable understanding that you cannot live on another man's revelation. What a lesson, indeed! Believing that someone else's relationship with the Lord is more important than your own is a snare.

In this situation, that was exactly what happened, as you will read in the pages ahead. The mistake I made of placing another man's relationship with the Lord higher than both my own relationship with God and my relationships with those around me was mostly because of Mr. Leader's amazing ability to prophesy into the lives of people. Surely, he had a special connection with God! Therefore, my incorrect response was to step and fetch for whatever this man wanted.

There is a great lesson to be learned here: the principle of knowing your lane. Your lane is just as important as another person's lane. When it comes to leadership, however, it is of the utmost importance for every leader to recognize precisely that for which he or she is graced. If any leader forms a lane that they desire to function in, but are not truly supposed to be in, they run the risk of becoming empowered in that lane. The results of this empowerment can be disastrous.

A leader empowered in the wrong lane will often start out well, but when their capacity to function in this area becomes exceeded by what is demanded of the position, the leader can become a villain, or look like the bad guy. They can become hostile, toxic or even abusive, all due to their inability to recognize where their own capacity has hit a ceiling.

In addition, they demand everyone else in the organization remain under the limits of their own capacity. In a desperate attempt at self-preservation, they are unable to relinquish control to another who is graced by God to fulfill those assignments, as though they must force their own relevance. Self-preservation is suffocating. Like a drowning person, those who succumb to it drag down any who try to rescue them out of a frantic selfishness.

The sad part is that many people never surrender to the notion of empowering others. The subtle reward to empowering others is cloaked by the self-preservation of insecure leaders.

A leader who is intimidated by others, fearing that the gifts of their subordinates might surpass their own, will try to keep others down. They will overlook the benefits of empowering people to excel in the lanes they were created for.

They are completely unable to recognize the reward of empowerment that is life for not only the empowered, but the leader as well! When a leader empowers others in the lane for which they are best suited, everyone wins because it builds a true team.

When this is in place, a leader—even one with little ability alone—can rise together with a team of empowered individuals. That is really living, as opposed to succumbing to the self-centeredness of control.

However, these leaders miss out on the truth that empowering others is the path to incredible reward! At first, investing in others may seem to only carry a small reward, so the need for self-preservation will cause a leader to miss out on the great reward that comes from developing other people.

By setting aside this fear of losing one's own position, and building others, a leader can leave behind an incredible legacy of empowered lives!

My mistake was misidentifying the capacity of the leader I served. I thought that Mr. Leader could grow past certain mechanisms of self-preservation he had lightly displayed in the beginning. I convinced myself, beyond discernment and emotional intelligence, based on the wow factor of his amazing gift. This was an error, likely due to the father void in me that created a deep need to please anyone I deemed worthy.

The view of the circumstances, through my intentionally biased lens, was that Mr. Leader could be changed and possessed far greater capacity than all the facts indicated. I told myself that he just needed to realize it, sincerely desiring that he would become a globally recognized voice.

Even when there were signs in the early days of flawed character and double standards, I remained at his side out of loyalty and a true desire to see this hero of mine win.

Culture of Perfectionism

Unfortunately, I found myself involved in a culture of extreme perfectionism. Mr. Leader possessed a very dominating presence which was amplified by his ability to consistently share jaw-dropping prophecies more clearly, and with more "freakish accuracy" than anyone I have ever seen, to this day.

This prophetic gift is what initially captured my attention. In fact, the reason it was so captivating was due to a sense of familiarity. His experiences with the Voice of God greatly resonated with my own history with the supernatural.

The same type of things had happened to me, and through me, from a very young age. Part of the allure to being around this type of person is that it actually made me feel normal. For the first time in my life, I wasn't alone!

He would share remarkable details about the lives of people, even their names, occupations, and information about their family members. Mr. Leader predicted the exact numbers where the stock market would be at annually for seven years in a row. As a result, there were many interested business leaders who would attend this organization's functions. He also predicted the election of presidents and leaders, in the United States and other nations as well.

That alone was impressive, but he would also declare what percentage points they would win by! Over the years, these consistent prophetic accuracies placed him and our team in a variety of international political settings, as well as stadium events in different parts of the world.

Mr. Leader would minister to people with tenacity and, most often, a heart of love. Countless people would burst into tears as they were set free from emotional pain, or given valuable supernatural information regarding how to navigate very serious scenarios.

As implied earlier, being a part of this setting caused a deep loyalty to arise within me—specifically toward Mr. Leader. I suppose that during those days there was a missing piece within me which made me willing to do anything and everything for him and his organization. After all, I had found my tribe and a very gifted leader! His amazing results made it easier to overlook the negatives.

Months turned into years as I developed under Mr. Leader's mentorship. My natural gifting grew exponentially. Dreams had always been a part of my journey, but they became far clearer. In this time, the things I dreamt about—involving names, locations and very specific information—would often come to pass within a day or a week. Another thing that developed that while praying for people, their names and other detailed information about their lives would come to me.

The training of this organization focused on leveraging the gifting within me to see things in people's lives as well as global events. The main thrust of the organization was specifically prophecy through words of knowledge, and future predictions.

This ability was sharpened non-stop for sixteen years. In many ways, this was a good thing. Yet, it was also a dysfunction because it was the sole purpose of the organization's existence, and the only purpose of Mr. Leader.

There was very little Gospel teaching. Instead, there was always a focus on a new prophetic word. The value was never placed on the simplicity of the Bible, but always on a new revelation. This was fine in the beginning, as the intentions seemed to be upright. However, Mr. Leader's—

and the organization's—capacity was challenged as more and more people from around the world began to participate.

The Season Progressed

So, there we were, in a season of intense ministry training: in the prophetic, international ministry, television, and hosting conferences. This was training like never before. We were building TV studios, participating in hours of production, and conducting live broadcasted meetings on a global stage. All while also hosting prophetic training conferences all over the world. I was absolutely convinced that serving at all costs was the way to be promoted before the Lord, regardless of the time or sacrifice to my family. I was determined to serve better than anyone.

My gifts were growing, and my serving was so intense, that a culture was set in the organization by my standard of servitude. People were blessed by the long hours of ministry. Mr. Leader was blessed by all the acts of service the team and I would do on the side, such as mowing the lawn, washing cars, running daylong errands at a whim, making sure that we never went to any other meeting other than what he approved, enthusiastically showing up for impromptu (endless) administrative meetings, cutting off any friends of which he didn't approve, and even handling any confrontation for him by dismissing people he no longer wanted to be in relationship with.

It was so important to me to honor Mr. Leader that any time we had extra money, including student loans, we would give it to him for whatever he wanted. For many of these years, we lived either in friends' basements, or in small, low-end apartments. It eventually became very difficult to make ends meet because my commitment was all-consuming.

For the years that I attended a university, majoring in biblical studies, it was almost crushing with full-time college credits, full-time construction work, and serving several hours per day as a requirement of the organization. Additionally, full commitments were required to attend events hosted by the organization most weekends. We had to balance all of this with one vehicle and two small children. Regardless of the demand, we found a way to make it work at that pace for the majority of those sixteen years.

We were eventually told that it had become our responsibility to raise our own resources to work full-time at the organization. Ultimately, we did this by going out under the strict permission of Mr. Leader to minister in other locations. Sometimes we had to cancel any event we had booked, even at the last moment, if something came up that was more important to him.

Ultimately, we were forced onto government assistance for food. We were always under the expectation that right around the corner would come a major breakthrough and that all our needs would be abundantly met by the organization.

This was motivation enough to muscle through the humiliation of living on assistance while pulling 80 plus hour weeks for many years, with little to no time off. In the first twenty years of our marriage we never took a vacation because we were unable to afford it. And for sixteen years there was never any time allotted for us to be absent from the organization.

What started out as fun and exciting eventually ground into a toxic and abusive environment.

Heather went along with my desire to remain at this organization. However, toward the last few years, she voiced her desire to leave. She was never in full agreement to remain there as long as we did, but it was the path I felt necessary for us to keep following.

In the beginning, it was a good experience. The lesson in it all was that sometimes when organizations, people, or teams grow past their capacity, they become unstable and even damaging. This ultimately became the case for both Mr. Leader and the organization.

For context, this organization was small in scale at the beginning, but grew rapidly when friends and family who had been a part of ministry with me in the past followed me to it. They, too, were wowed by the awesome display of the prophetic in action. Together, we saw many lives impacted for God. Everyone felt privileged to be a part of this very unique organization. It was orderly and constantly becoming more perfected. Things started out with striving for excellence, but grew into a demand for absolute perfection, defined by the words "order" and "protocol".

Alongside our high emphasis on prophetic ministry, etiquette and how to work with leaders in the church, the government, and the marketplace was emphasized daily. These were very good things to learn, but in this scenario, they were all subjective and defined by Mr. Leader, whose expectations were constantly changing.

Things evolved to a point that if people broke some of the rules that really had no measurable guidelines, they were scolded under the premise of teaching them how to behave. This always brought about a sickening sense inside of me. But being young and agreeing to be mentored, I chose to attempt to learn rather than question, all while believing that Mr. Leader knew better than anyone. This ultimately fostered a harsh, pharisaical attitude in myself and the entire team.

Fire Hammer

One memory of the intense pharisaical composure concerns a promotional flyer we put out for an international event we were hosting in Europe. Some of the people in our organization thought we should name our band "Fire Hammer" because of Jeremiah 23:29, which says, *"'Is not my word like fire,' declares the LORD, 'and like a hammer that breaks a rock in pieces?'"* (NIV).

The picture of our band looked like a bunch of mean jerks staring down the camera—no joke! I heavily disagreed with the name and protested, "This band will sound like some kind of death metal group! No, we are not naming our worship band 'Fire Hammer.'" To this day, many of the former friends involved still joke with me about Fire Hammer, saying things like, "You sure fire hammered that one!" And, "Let's really fire hammer this meeting!" Wow...

I quickly became one of the most prominent figures in the organization. As such, my respect and loyalty for Mr. Leader only became more and more unshakable. When we first began participating on a full-time basis, there were other people who had a quiet eagerness to leave. They would discretely pull me aside and share their concerns with how things were and that they could no longer participate. My response was always dismissal, refusing to hear anything negative about Mr. Leader. I would think to myself, *These people just don't know how great he is and how much God is with him.*

"Be Careful, He Reads Minds"

The culture of the organization eventually grew into a place centered around Mr. Leader's personality and wishes. In principle, this is not necessarily wrong. However, one of the prevailing things that began to grow as part of the fabric of the team was that Mr. Leader was so prophetically strong that he would know our thoughts.

This should have been a red flag much sooner. However, it was taught in a casual way and implied that it was all part of the operation of his gift. Couple that with constantly seeing leaders from various parts of the world coming to meet with him due to the mind-blowing accuracy of his ability, and it definitely left the door open to the strong possibility that he may, at times, be passively reading your mind! The culture of this organization encouraged and reinforced this notion.

We were young, and honestly so filled with faith and willingness to serve that the initial thoughts were, *Of course! Yes, this is God's prophet and we have the privilege to be a part of something truly special and unique. After all, not many places have a leader that can hear people's thoughts!*

You Need a Father

Over time, a heavy emphasis was placed on "spiritual fathering". We brought people in for meetings and asked them, "Who is your daddy?" We would tell them that they need a father and that's why they weren't yet where they needed to be. Although there is truth in this to a degree, when implemented in a healthy way, it was executed with the wrong application. It was the job of our team to guide anyone interested in joining up to accept Mr. Leader as their spiritual father and that they were a son/daughter of the house. This came with high expectations of what was required of them.

A small leadership group, including me, oversaw the vetting of anyone who wanted to join our team. For each candidate, we read through several pages of very detailed (and some pretty unbelievable) personal information to determine if he or she would be a good fit. It was also my responsibility, along with one other team member, to let people go or make sure they were keeping the requirements of the organization.

No one was ever excused from our weekly, sometimes daily, meetings. If there was a scheduling conflict, the team member would potentially have to miss work and family functions such as birthdays, anniversaries, weddings, graduations, and other special events. The only exceptions were an immediate family member's funeral or wedding.

Team members were especially forbidden to go to other meetings or participate in other ministry functions without direct permission from our main office. The team was never allowed to gather in a group of more than three people outside the organization's regularly scheduled times. If they did, it was considered a meeting that needed to be approved by the office on a first-come request basis.

If they gathered without permission, we would bring them in and talk to them. If it continued, they were off the team. When any team member had a fallout with Mr. Leader, they would either leave the organization or be asked to leave. Additionally, anyone who was no longer on the team, or in good standing with Mr. Leader, would be blocked on all forms of social media. The team and staff were also required to block, unfriend and no longer have any contact with anyone who was no longer a part of the organization.

The Later It Gets, the Earlier It Gets

The organization was known for holding ridiculously long meetings. People arrived around four o'clock in the afternoon with the actual meeting time starting close to seven o'clock in the evening. We often left the meeting place anywhere from four o'clock to eight o'clock in the morning. People stayed because of the legitimate prophetic gifting they experienced. Many lives were dramatically changed and rescued as a result of the prophetic ministry that was in action at these meetings. However, the internal culture of organization continued to become more stringent.

There came a point when we would hold a series of meetings that lasted nearly two months at a time. During these two months, it was not uncommon to only get one or two days off. Many team members went to work in the morning after the meeting ended, sometimes sleeping and changing clothes in their cars. S

ome team members slept in the sound area with all the camera gear. Some people were in college, others held regular jobs, and the strain was tremendous. If you missed one meeting without permission, you received a warning and became potentially benched. If it happened twice, you were off the team.

Mr. Leader was one of the most gifted people I have ever met. But over time, he became toxic. One day, everything was wonderful and the most amazing work environment ever, the following day (sometimes the following hour) there was a sudden, illogical change of mood. There would be an eruption of anger or scolding of team members that was out of the blue and irrational.

On international trips, in any hotel we stayed at, the executive director of the ministry would not allow anyone to have a room on a floor higher than Mr. Leader. If guests or individuals who financially supported the organization ever traveled along with the team and booked a room on a floor higher than his, it was demanded of them that they change to a floor lower than the prophet.

If any one of these high-level hotels failed to meet any of Mr. Leader's expectations, the entire management staff would be called into the lobby and harshly scolded. At times, while going through customs, if the check through time took too long, he would shout at the top of his lungs, "This is taking too long! I will get one of the leaders in government that I know here and correct this unacceptable situation!"

Sometimes, he demanded to see the manager of an entire international airport and would not leave until he was able to educate them on how to properly run an organization. It was moments like these that began the change in my heart. I started to realize this was not a healthy place to be.

The Beginning of the End

Things greatly changed during a season of our tenure when, only a few months apart, two key team members suddenly died. It was deeply troubling to me that a few weeks after the deaths, the spouse of one of the team members was scolded for being sad and sulking around. The grieving spouse was told, "That is enough! No one wants to see all your negativity. I won't tolerate it anymore!" He demanded that this individual stop bringing everyone else down.

Other members began to have physical issues, and people left the organization after being rocked by the death of one of our most beloved members. The overwhelming and unsustainable schedule was also a contributing factor. It is hard to say, but both deaths and much of the physical ailments were definitely not helped by the rigorous schedule that the organization demanded.

The beginning of the end came when, early one morning, I had a dream. In it, I was dressed in a typical three-piece suit that was average dress code for the organization. Heather and both of my children, Alison and Daniel, were with me. While leading them to a room, we walked past Mr. Leader and a number of people who were new faces coming into the organization.

They were all wowed by my dedication while Mr. Leader watched with curiosity as we walked past them into a far back room. In this back room, the four of us took a seat. The walls were concrete, and we were now wearing dressy travel jackets over the dress clothes typically worn at meetings.

The kids and Heather were facing me on the other side of the small room, all of us sitting on concrete benches. Suddenly to my left, the concrete wall lifted to reveal a glass wall. Behind it was a raging fire like a blast furnace. It was terrifying! We could feel the heat through our heavy winter travel jackets. I assured my family that this was good, and everything was going to be alright. I told them it was a good decision that we were doing this and that it would all be over soon. We all knew that the glass wall was about to lift up and the blasting fire would explode into the room we were sitting in, consuming us to the point of death.

However, before the glass lifted, something prompted me to stand up and walk out. As I did so, I met the group and Mr. Leader in the other room once again. "This isn't right, we have to go." I said. They protested, but he knew what we were doing was correct. Yet, he wouldn't say it out loud.

It was real and terrifying! For the longest time I thought it was a vision of hell. What took place after that dream confirmed its real meaning and was a catalyst to make a transition.

Exposure of Wrong Priorities

As I mentioned before, we were eventually told we had to go outside our regular meeting times to raise financial support for ourselves. Whereas at first it was challenging, as soon as we began holding meetings of our own, our financial situation began to turn around. It was difficult but we did what it took.

For a year, I helped a church in a different state a couple times a month, filling their pulpit until they found a new pastor. This required leaving our meeting place on a Saturday night after speaking, and driving all night to make their Sunday morning service.

I would preach the morning service, minister to people in the congregation, meet with leaders in the afternoon, then do their night service. Afterwards, I either collapsed in a hotel or pushed through all the way back home.

I conducted weekly meetings in locations several hours away, as well as additional monthly meetings in different states through many of the relationships we developed before our time at the organization.

Through these meetings, many things began to break through. We had always been givers with whatever we had. We had sown cars and finances to many people over the years and once we stepped out, it came back in a major harvest.

Within a year or two of doing this, we had a new home paid for and a new vehicle. It was a Mercedes ministry van with a trailer, tv gear, sound system, and a lot of other awesome things!

Heather Becomes Ill

During one of our special meetings, Heather became seriously ill. Her eyes and face swelled. She was barely able to function or even get out of bed. We were so used to being exhausted, but it seemed she was a little more tired than usual. Leading up to this, she was required to not miss one meeting because it was demanded by the leadership that she open the meetings because she was powerful, and the attendees were greatly impacted by her presence.

At this particular special meeting, she nearly collapsed on the platform. This caused something to change in me, and I declared, "I'm leaving the meeting with her!" I took Heather to the emergency room to discover both of her kidneys had failed due to hereditary renal disease. It was horrible. Even more so because I realized that it was my blind sense of loyalty which caused inexcusable negligence toward my wife's well-being.

Memories, tainted with regret, flooded my mind. I recalled a time, years earlier, while at one of the ministry's meetings, when Heather was pregnant with our first child. I was doing music and needed to do another special song during the service when suddenly Heather's water broke! Her sister, who was attending that particular meeting, told me, "She needs to go in right now!"

My response (out of duty to the service) was, "Do you think you can wait twenty more minutes?" I thought her sister was going to kill me—and rightly so! I did end up getting Heather to the hospital in time for a healthy delivery. It was this absence of priority, engrafted by the culture of this organization, that was astonishing and regretful.

Heather ended up being hospitalized for renal failure. Due to a few complications, the medical staff explained that this was very serious, and she could die. It went from this moment, to her being rushed into surgery to have a tube put in her heart. It was a brutal procedure because they used the wrong sized apparatus, and rather than getting the right size, they carved through the front part of her shoulder.

This was the beginning of a five-year battle for Heather's life. She was on dialysis for nearly three years, involving many surgeries which scarred her body.

We were thankful for the miracles that took place during that horrible season. Heather did ultimately receive a kidney transplant, and we will cover this story in more detail in the pages ahead.

As this all unfolded, Mr. Leader wrongly said that Heather was to blame for allowing this to happen to her body!

Now, if you are anything like me, you might be asking the question, "What was the matter with you, Joseph?! Why did you stay in this kind of place?" Well, as stated at the beginning of the chapter, I haven't included everything in this account. If I did, it would be much more understandable as to why we stayed for so long.

Teachings on submission I had heard in my younger years contributed to my loyalty. To defy your leadership was to defy God. As a result, it was bad teaching and wrong understanding of healthy authority which caused me to make my family endure these types of things.

I was being groomed to take over the whole organization. It was in my heart and mind that if I just hung on, there would be a day when Mr. Leader would step down, and I would be able to honor and protect him and protect the people from him. It seemed that the powerful gift he possessed was worth protecting because it had such an impact.

Healing

Heather began listening to a teacher named Andrew Wommack every day, for hours on end, while in dialysis and elsewhere. His teaching on the love and grace of God had already been impacting my life, but we were afraid to mention it.

One particular day, Heather began choking from the formation of blood clots in her neck. Her specialists said it was really serious and warned us the clots could go to her brain. She discovered that Andrew was doing a one night only special meeting in our city. Heather boldly told me that she was going to see Andrew Wommack rather than go to our meetings that night. I knew to agree with her.

She went there and sat through the entire service nearly choking. After the service was over, she felt prompted by the Holy Spirit to stay seated after everyone left. At the point when there was hardly anyone left in the auditorium, she looked up and saw Andrew at the stage area. An usher got her attention and waved her their way! She stood in front of Andrew, not able to speak well, but conveyed with tears what was happening.

Andrew replied, "Well, I don't know what you're saying, but God sure does." He began to pray over her, for healing and breaking off a spiritual attack as well. After leaving that meeting, Heather called me saying, "I'm healed!"

However, after examining her, the blood clots were still very much present. But I didn't dare say anything contrary to what she was saying! Two days later, she woke up, checked her neck, and the full manifestation of what she had been believing God for had happened: the blood clots were completely gone!

This made a tremendous impact on both of us. Maybe what we were living under needed to change.

Confronted by the Voice of God

This realization that a change was needed came to a head the day the Holy Spirit spoke to me. He said, "You have stepped into the fear of man and care more about what Mr. Leader thinks than what I have for you to do."

The dream of the blast furnace came back to me. This moment ripped my heart, and I cried out, "Lord, I don't know how to get out of this!" I had built conferences, training materials, and a Bible school for this organization. I had led dozens of friends, family and team members to become part of the very fabric of it.

"If I leave, they will all be stuck here."

However, the day came when we decided to leave. At first, upon realizing we were making this request, Mr. Leader was benevolent. But things slowly changed.

He announced, "If anyone who came here with Joseph and Heather want to join up with them, they are welcome to do so, only with my blessing." Eighty percent of the team made an appointment with him to get his blessing to go with us. It was hard all the way around. Some individuals who we didn't bring to the organization came to me and requested to come with me, but Heather and I refused because it didn't feel right.

There came a point when Mr. Leader demanded that anything we had of his be brought to his storage place. So, my team gathered everything we could and brought it there. Mr. Leader arrived unannounced and challenged one of my creative directors to a fist fight. We almost ended up having a physical altercation between members of his team and members of ours. It was so immature!

Leaving with Honor

Upon leaving, I made it clear that as an act of honor, no one in our ministry would tithe or financially support us. Instead, we all would support our former leader and organization for six months after leaving.

After fulfilling this commitment, the exact day we stopped tithing to this organization, we were all blocked on every form of social media and every other form of communication. The new members of the organization told everyone around us that if they were in contact with us that they could not be friends on social media or have any other form of contact. They were told that that I had personally plotted for years to destroy the former organization.

After leaving, we were approached by individuals who wanted to bless Heather and me. We discovered that more than one person was donating up to fifty-thousand dollars a month to that organization! We also found that there were many other forms of income they had been given as well. Yet, it was during the season that Heather and I were on food stamps so we could make the organization run, when we were told there weren't enough resources for us.

As time went on, memories of the early days, when the Voice of God spoke to me on the wind, would go through my mind. There was sadness at times, as it became clearer that this was not the journey God had first called me to.

However, all that mattered now was that we were out and free. What unfolded next was a changing point in my entire walk with the Lord.

Chapter Eight
Revelation of Jesus

Have you ever been passionate about something you knew you wanted but didn't know how to articulate it? That is the case for many people, but rather than continue through the pain and joy of discovery, they abandon that desire. It's not uncommon to see people start out with a passionate drive who end up settling. The wear and tear of pain, mixed with time, can drag anyone's passion to a halt. This was the case in our journey, especially after our break-away from sixteen years of dedicated service.

Let's start out by acknowledging how good it is to be irrationally passionate about something—something that is constructive and unique to you! Artists have that kind of fire to varying degrees. In any arena, it takes a great effort to achieve the rank of highest and best.

Consider the effort it takes to become a physician, to master a martial art, or become a jet pilot. Anything worth achieving takes passion and discipline. In my case, it has always been a challenge to live in the norm. I'm a dreamer.

Dreaming during much of my younger life was a way of escape. The stillness of being away from activity is how creativity flows. It wasn't until I was older and had taken in more of the Word of God, that I realized it was okay to make dreams a reality!

For many people, it's dreadful when what they start out enthusiastically pursuing takes longer than expected, or trials of life come out of nowhere. When we combine trials and time without the desired result, the recipe can produce doubt or hesitation.

It's Not the Age, It's the Mileage

It takes a special tenacity to go after your dreams without stopping. Over the years, the challenges of visionary living can cause weariness.

"It's not the years, honey. It's the mileage." — Indiana Jones, *Raiders of the Lost Ark*

There were a number of compounding factors that wore us down. Not only had we been in a pressure cooker of an organization for sixteen years, but our family was hit on many fronts.

Our son, Daniel, developed strange physical behaviors and became socially unresponsive. We didn't think much of it until we were visiting my friend, Ryan. His mom, Christine, kindly approached us after witnessing our son's behavior and suggested we get him evaluated for autism.

Having no background with that topic, we agreed. Heather took Daniel to the doctor and came home in tears. We discovered that he was highly autistic, in need of twelve specialists.

Through prayer and diligence, Daniel is now brilliantly functioning, with no specialists! We have a tremendous relationship with him. People don't realize there is anything different about him until he speaks, although his communication is great. Daniel is growing and gaining traction every day. For this, we praise God!

Our oldest child, Alison, was diagnosed with a genetic renal issue. At the time, we had no idea she had inherited it from her mom, as Heather's kidneys had not yet failed. Thankfully, we caught it at a young age and the necessary procedure was done.

However, Ali's recovery from the surgery wasn't easy. She developed dark circles under her eyes and crippling pain in her stomach, causing her to miss many school days. Heather and I continuously took her to the doctor, but they never found anything wrong. The school nurse even suggested that Ali was faking her pain to get out of school, which really frustrated us.

Then, during a season of an entire month of meetings, the cause of our little girl's pain was revealed when she passed a large amount of surgical gauze! We jarred it, in hopes of bringing it to the doctor, or possibly even an attorney.

In the meantime, our house was owned by Mr. Leader. As a result of him not arranging the required income, it was sold out from under us at the end of those month-long meetings. We were informed we had 24 hours to move before the new owners took possession of the house.

In the process of emergency packing with anyone who would help, the evidence of our daughter passing gauze was lost. Highly frustrated, we now had no physical evidence of what our little girl had suffered through for nearly a year. It was shortly after this when Heather fell deathly ill.

During our transition from the former organization, Heather was in dialysis three days a week. She didn't qualify to receive a kidney from the national transplant list, due to the high levels of antibodies in her blood. In spite of this, a friend led of the Holy Spirit went to the doctor to see if she was a match for Heather; unfortunately, she was not.

Yet, through a program called the Paired Donor Exchange, a miracle match was made. Outside of Minnesota, there were two other patients also awaiting kidney transplant. Each of them had an individual who volunteered to be donors, yet were not compatible with the patients they wanted to help. Through this program, all three were matched with another patient, including Heather!

Heather's kidney was emergency flown from out of state to our hospital in Minnesota and our friend's kidney was given to another patient across state lines as well. We later discovered that Heather's kidney came from a large man from Georgia. Heather is just over five-foot-one, so it was a massive kidney for her! And I kid you not—during her recovery, she behaved differently than the lady I married! She ordered hot wings and shouted at UFC all night. What a sight!

However, this same period of time proved fruitful in that the ministry we established grew rapidly to the point where we had three growing church campuses, each in different states. This required a weekly broadcast by which we were able to hold live services that simultaneously reached all the campuses.

We had also developed a traveling system to minister to people all over the country. Our team held seventy-eight live meetings per year where I spoke on location from different cities and states. In addition, we had other weekly meetings and speaking engagements, a variety of conferences annually, and had built an online Bible college. It was all a tremendous endeavor. The Bible school alone had a few hundred people go through the two years of training.

The responsibility of this season had quadrupled from the previous, and even after her transplant, Heather was continually fighting to be well. We loved each other and just wanted to be able to keep functioning with all the opportunity that was in front of us. After a few years of doing this, I resorted to running on autopilot, just functioning to keep the machine—that I had created—running.

Why Am I Doing This?

I remember that for years, even before Heather and I were married, I often asked myself this dramatic question, "Why am I doing this to myself?!" It's as if I refused to have a normal life. Always in the Word, frequently in solitude and seeking out ministers who would teach me church history and how to study the Bible, etc. I knew I had something inside me that was being matured and seasoned for a future time. This held me back from doing things everyone else did or thought I should be doing. I was responsible and worked hard but never "bought in" all the way to anything other than what was happening on the inside. The only place that brought a sense of normalcy was opening the Bible, reading it, and talking to God.

I would think, *It seems like everyone I know is establishing careers, buying houses, and moving on in life.* Yet, in the middle of that thought, I would continue nurturing the drive inside, the need to feed the intense craving for knowledge of God and His Word.

This craving went well beyond a Sunday morning church goer or someone who just got back from a conference. I was one who wanted to leave it all behind, no matter the cost, to assuage this one burning motivation on the inside: to know the truth and somehow leave a mark of significance in this life.

I recognized that this life is temporary, so I asked myself, *What will remain? What is the point?*

Through this time, most everyone who knew me loved my sincerity, but had no expectation for me to achieve anything significant. I could feel it. I knew I was liked and loved, but lived so uniquely that it caused most people to relegate me into a category marked, "That's just Joe Z."

People were intrigued with me, "What are you about? Why do you burn the way you do?" During those early years, I was not capable of effectively communicating what I wanted, let alone where I was going. My best response was usually, "Because I have to."

The idea of doing the normal nine-to-five life was soul-crushing. Not because of the work; on the contrary, life was filled with hard work. I poured my best efforts into every place that employed me, resulting in many promotions and offers for advancement.

During my university days, especially in biblical studies, I was at the top of my class. However, at every turn, there was a burning sense of a destination that was beyond explanation, and it was exhausting. This led to the dramatic question over and over again, "Why am I doing this to myself?"

Years after Heather and I were married, she would look at me and say, "You know you're a gypsy?"

I would respond in good humor, "What?"

"You're a gypsy," she would say again.

At the time, I didn't know what she meant. Later, I discovered she wasn't referring to any of the negative things related to gypsies, but that she was lightheartedly pointing out my need to go and find: the thrilling inspiration to build and create, to make a difference in social structures by bringing people together for a purpose, large or small.

My friends would often say, "You should be a politician because of the way you care about people and your deep-rooted desire to move them toward greatness."

Heather was right; gypsy was a fair description as it related to my desire to live outside the box. However, living outside the box, without being effective in moving toward an ultimate purpose and destination, was pointless. I know God put that on the inside of me: to be both outside the box and highly effective. The question was, "How?" One morning, the answer came.

What Do You See?

One early Minnesota fall morning, the sun was barely breaking the horizon. A familiar Voice rose up in my heart, the unction of the Holy Spirit, the Voice of God. It had been a long, painful season, and it had been quite a bit of time since I had heard His Voice so clearly. It was subtle, but unmistakably His familiar Voice.

The Voice manifested this time as an inner prompting to go outside and take a walk. So, that's I did, putting shoes and sweatshirt on, then walking out the door at a good pace. The air smelled fresh, the ground was misty, and a light fog hovered at the base of the tree lines in the distance.

After walking for a while, my feet found a small trail through a tiny thicket and the unction pulled at me to follow it. I hadn't walked many steps before I came out to the edge of a freshly tilled field.

I stood motionless for a moment, when the question arose from the Voice of God, "What do you see?" For a brief moment, I paused, then exhaled and said, "A plowed field."

Not thinking much about this exchange, after another pause, I calmly turned to walk away. His voice came again, saying, "Go back, and look again."

I replied, "Yes, Sir." This made me pay attention because of His request that I go back. Once again, standing at the end of the short, wooded path on the border of that tilled field, I looked more intently across it.

There were no more questions, only a statement that welled up inside of me with peace and assurance. "As far as your eyes can see, I have called you to reach the masses and build lives by My Word." I was flooded with a deep knowing that the Voice of God had spoken to me. Suddenly, my mind opened to the image of millions of people in this field and beyond.

A relaxed intensity settled within and I responded, "Yes, Sir."

Walking back, many thoughts of how to do this flooded through my mind. The realization arose that this vision was in reference to the mandate on my life. *I have to make disciples through media. The highest use of the Voice of God in my life is to speak through media. This is where my responsibility as a prophet functions.*

Prophetic Confirmations

While walking, the Holy Spirit reminded me of an encounter that had taken place seven years earlier while on an overseas trip to Norway. A group of us were hosting a prophetic conference and ministering to global business leaders. After a heavy day, we all gathered at our hotel in Oslo. While we all stood together in one of the rooms to pray, the power of God came on me and knocked me to the ground.

I fell down like a dead person and saw into the realm of the spirit. I saw nations and continents with leaders and many other people being influenced. There was a particular man of high influence who was waiting to hear from us, similar to Paul's dream of the Macedonian man saying, "Come here and help us!" It was all so real to me, I became overwhelmed with emotion.

There was a moment when a large, red letter A was written in the air. The Lord spoke, "I've called you to an apostolic ministry that will establish and reach the masses."

There was a prayer warrior with me, and as I fell into a dramatic trance, he was also overcome by the Spirit of God. As I was seeing these things, he simultaneously received a vision and prophesied to the same man as in my vision, confirming much of what I had just seen! It was intense for us both.

That was one of the few times in my life where the power of God was so strong it was nearly palpable. This was a calling the Lord placed on my life for apostolic ministry. By definition, as it applies to me, this means a builder, or a way-maker, not only for my specific mandate, but so that others can run down a cut path to also reach the globe.

Years later, a dream came to me. In this dream, I was with a few of the people I had raised up in ministry. We were clearing a trail in the cold, cutting down trees and clearing paths. Finally, after a great deal of sweaty, diligent work, we had labored enough to make a clearing for a pathway down a long hill. We continued right up to the point where the pathway had become recognizable as a sledding hill that went a good distance.

A guy trained under me stepped up wearing a travel coat and holding a briefcase. He looked comfortable and cool, as if he had been relaxing and waiting for his cue to arrive. He sat down on the sled we had laid at the top of the path, his blank face completely oblivious to how much work we had just put into this project. Yet, he was waiting for me to push him!

This took me aback, as I thought, *What an ungrateful person! We are not even being acknowledged for what we did!* However, I got behind him, with a little reservation, and pushed him down the hill.

After waking, it became clear to me that we would walk through many trials, and it would take a lot of hard work for my mandate and gifting to clear the way for the Gospel to be spread around the world. However, many others would utilize the smooth path without ever fully understanding whom God had used to build it. It was kind of the Lord's way of saying, "Get over yourself!"

God had spoken to me about reaching the masses and what some of that model would look like, and there was a lot of ministry happening as a result. However, there was a missing piece in me that had to be resolved by the Lord before the revelation and mandate could be fully realized.

Reconnecting with Dave Duell

One of the most pivotal points came when Dave Duell and I reconnected after many years. Dave was holding a meeting in Wisconsin, and we were able to attend. After our time with him, Dave invited our family to see him in

Colorado. We decided it was important and made plans to take a trip to Colorado.

After spending a few days ministering at their church and hanging out together, Dave and his wife, Bonnie, invited us to their men's conference a few months later in Buena Vista, Colorado. We had a strong sense that we should attend, so we cleared our schedule, as this was a priority, and decided to bring our entire team along. Heather also came and hung out with a group of the ladies involved in Dave and Bonnie's ministry.

This conference was the second time Dave Duell's ministry greatly impacted my life. There was nothing profound about the conference itself, although we had the privilege of meeting many great guys. However, the significance of this meeting was realized during one of the sessions.

A Revelation Of Jesus

One of the leaders at the event stood up to lead us in communion. As he talked, something shifted inside my heart, uncomfortable and invasive. My emotions became overwhelmed as the Holy Spirit flooded my whole person. Listening to grace revelation speakers over these few days evoked tears. I wasn't sad, but tears flowed uncontrollably. As the sessions carried on, something unlocked inside me.

The Holy Spirit captured my attention, my emotions, my ambitions and everything in between. The only thing I was able to communicate was tears. After years of being in a hard-core ministry organization, this was foreign—very foreign! But once the tears started, they continued at every session for nearly two days! It was embarrassing and hard to control.

Some of the guys from my team stared at me, "Hey, Z—are you alright?" My uncle Paul, who at the time was the senate majority leader of the Republican party in Minnesota, had also accompanied me. He laid hands on me, prayed over me, and blessed me. It was a tremendous moment.

When the event was over, I asked God, "What was that all about?" The answer came to me, "Those were the tears of a Pharisee, and you were being cleansed." This was an encounter with the real Jesus.

Galatians 1:12 refers to this as the revelation of Jesus. This is why the Apostle Paul was so bold in preaching the Word of God! He was operating in a revelation of Jesus through encountering Him! My tears were a result of the Holy Spirit cleansing me from self-righteousness and performance-based religion, acquired by my own intensity as well as those sixteen years with that former organization.

Something changed in me that day! With a love and compassion for people unlike ever before, my preaching and teaching of the Word became very different. In fact, one of my dear friends listened to some of my teachings from many years back and noted a major shift from my earlier, edgy harshness to a sweetness and spirit of grace. The years of secretly listening to Andrew Wommack's teaching, along with this encounter, culminated in an intense revelation that I was loved, which flowed out of me in ministry to others!

The Complete Gospel

It wasn't long after this when the Voice of God came to me again.

"I want you to preach the Complete Gospel." Not understanding what that even meant, my answer was, "Yes!"

I always had a legitimate mandate from God to "Go," but without this revelation, I would not have fully accomplished what God had in store. I needed a revelation of Jesus.

A revelation of Jesus is one of the number one reasons anyone should preach the Gospel! This is a common saying in our lives today: "There is a great difference between someone with a word from God versus someone with a good idea." A revelation of Jesus is equivalent to having a word from God to do something. It's like a rite of passage. This is what happened to me at that conference in Buena Vista, Colorado.

The Complete Gospel isn't anything new; the Gospel of Jesus Christ is the only Gospel there is! However, what the Lord wanted me to preach was predicated on my deliverance from being a Pharisee.

I explain the Complete Gospel this way, "The Gospel you hear preached is correct, but it's not complete until it's working through you."

Thus, the Complete Gospel is the Gospel of Jesus Christ fully working through you. It's not a religion; it's not a philosophy or doctrine. It is the Gospel personally manifested in power through your life.

If you are flowing in the Completeness of the Gospel, then your life will demand an explanation.

Our walk was no longer about gifting or prophesying, but about the finished work of Jesus. The gifts that flowed as a result was God loving people through us! What a different way of seeing things!

Chapter Nine

Outcast Into A Broadcast

Our ministry team developed into a well-oiled machine, a traveling production, hosting as many as five conferences a year, in addition to our other speaking engagements. After receiving the word to reach the masses, a fire was lit in me to do so at any cost. The momentum of staff and volunteers was only increasing as the demands of travel and excellent production grew. The goal was to get on TV, in addition to everything else we had going on.

Our little ministry brought in hundreds of thousands of dollars that went right back into our monthly budget as fast as it came in. In hindsight, one mistake we made was paying the staff, and even volunteers, more than the ministry should have. We simply didn't want to repeat our own experiences from former days. As far as we were concerned, no one on *this* team was going to be on government assistance!

We joyfully gave our team members personal vehicles and many other various gifts and bonuses. During Heather's surgeries and recovery, we would come home to team members sleeping on our couch. All the rooms in our home were filled with team members living with us. We felt like we had an obligation to share everything we had with anyone connected to us.

We hosted Thanksgiving dinners, celebrated every holiday, and had special occasions when we would take the team out to dinner. Everyone knew we would always take care of every meal when they traveled with us. Our dinner bill averaged in the hundreds of dollars, and sometimes much more, often several times a week.

It was our goal to make sure anyone working for the kingdom of God as a part of our crew felt privileged to be with us. Sadly, it created an entitlement attitude within some members of our team. There were definitely some who gave their hearts and souls, asking nothing in return, but Heather and I certainly overdid it. That is no one's responsibility but our own.

Amish Invasion

For several years leading up to this decision, we were uniquely ministering to a large community of Amish. Auction halls were being rented out and packed with hundreds of Amish. In the beginning, we were asked to minister in the upper room of a barn meeting, a secret Amish gathering. They were curious about the operation of the gifts of the Spirit. Now, if you have five Amish in a meeting outside of their community, that is a crusade, but in this upper room, there were roughly seventy of them!

Teaching from a white board, I explained the different biblical dispensations of time. The purpose was to show them that we are in an age of grace that Jesus paid for and that they were welcome to participate by making Him the Lord of their lives.

Halfway through my teaching, the Holy Spirit spoke to me, "Tell them your testimony. Tell them about what it cost you to follow me. Tell them about your dad. Tell them about you leaving it all behind." My first thought was, *I don't want to!* That is not something that is comfortable to talk about.

The direction came strongly again, so I shifted gears to the story of choosing God over family. What a vulnerable feeling! After I shared the events of my journey, the place was still. Then the Holy Spirit moved on me to look at people in the audience, point them out, and share detailed information about their lives and what the Lord wanted to say to them.

After another moment of stillness, one man far in the back stood up, gripping his hair. With tears streaming down his face, he shouted, "I want Jesus!" Then shouted it again, "I want Jesus!"

More of them stood up and shouted the same thing! I fell on my knees and wept as the audience stood and all called out for Jesus to save them.

I stood to my feet, wiping tears away, and asked them, "Would you like to have the baptism of the Holy Spirit?" Instantly, they all shouted, "Yes!" But before I could even begin to lead them in the prayer to receive the baptism, some of them began to spontaneously speak in tongues. It grew into more and more until nearly all of them were loudly speaking in tongues! Tears gushed down my face as I witnessed this purity and hunger for the Lord.

This moment turned into years of meetings and hundreds of Amish getting born again! At first, we were celebrated, but later, jealousy and anger toward us grew. Our meetings were exciting! Other leaders said, "Don't allow any of your Amish people to go to those Joe Z meetings or they will take off their head coverings in five minutes flat!" Of course, my goal was never to change people's looks or behavior. It was simply to introduce them to Jesus and the power of the Holy Spirit, ultimately making them disciples and mature believers in the Word of God.

In that community, we made a terrible discovery. What seemed like nine out of ten of these Amish girls had been abused by a close relative. Heather ministered to many of them. In general, our hearts for these people were broken, and we fell in love with them.

Much of the church we established was out of the desire to give them a place to grow without being pulled back into some other form of bondage. The congregation was nearly half former Amish. You wouldn't know it because they all dressed like us. They were good people.

The Decision to Move

There came a point when it was difficult to keep up with visiting the three church groups in addition to traveling all over the country. A decision had to be made about how to continue. After several months of processing, we chose to consolidate the groups from Minnesota, Indiana and Ohio to the Indiana location, since it was more centrally located.

The leaders from Ohio wanted to move to Indiana and work with us from there to build outward. We kept the Minnesota campus open, but as a second location, rather than the first.

The team we had assembled, some of whom had been with us for 20 years, unanimously decided that they did not want to remain behind in Minneapolis. They insisted on going with us to Indiana to establish the work with the

Amish and continue building a global presence. The decision was made and we, along with nearly forty people, made the move to Indiana.

This was an exciting adventure. We had a tremendous time remodeling our home and building the church. I placed leaders in our various church campus locations in order of who had a better gift to pastor than I did, and they brought life to the community. We were also financially being blessed. There were business leaders in the community who were greatly impacted by the work we were doing. They saw their family members being changed for the good, and we had supporters from all over the country. It was a thrilling time.

Mixed Signals

The whole picture changed when Luke[3], one of the key leaders I was working with (who was formerly Amish) said that my preaching was hurting people and needed to be adjusted. Not being a native of the culture, I was quick to listen. I submitted to his counsel to the point that when speaking, I would ask anyone I may have offended to please forgive me. This went on for a few months. The people often looked puzzled by it, but my trusted friend was telling me "inside information," so my sense of responsibility said, "Do your best to make sure everyone is good."

One day, another one of the men came to me. He was one of the greatest men of integrity I had ever met, and formerly an Amish bishop. He said, "Stop apologizing! Who is in your head that you feel the need to be so careful?"

---

[3] This name has been changed to maintain confidentiality.

"Well, my friend, Luke." I responded. "He really knows what the people are saying."

He came right back at me with, "If he is saying this stuff to you, he is not your friend. There is no issue!"

This was puzzling to me because Luke was of a high reputation in the community and had become very involved in our ministry.

Things progressed normally until Luke finally said he thought it was best if he no longer sat in the front row. He said it seemed better for him to not be in view. This seemed strange to me, but not knowing what to say, and having a big heart for him, I agreed to whatever he thought was best.

Later on, seeing him in the back row, many of the other leaders began to sit with him as well, all the way against the back wall. Instead, newer people filled the front rows.

It was strange.

A Cascade of Tragic Events

Shortly following this strange shift, a cascade of tragic events came down all around us. It began while on one of my international trips. Luke got ahold of me while I was there for twenty-two days of ministry. He informed me that he wanted to step back completely from the church and ministry.

Now, he was a heavy giver and had done an immense amount of hard work to see everything we were doing together come alive in this particular community. He was a genuinely good guy! It was all very shocking to me.

I asked him, "Have I done something to offend you? Are you hurt? Why are you pulling back?" He said that it was due to how I was preaching and that he thought it was better for him to step aside. He also said if others asked him why, he would tell them that it was what he needed to do, and if they also wanted to leave, that it was up to them.

I said, "Okay, sounds like you will have your own thing going in no time. God bless you, man. Do what you have to do." I tried joking with him and keeping it light because of my genuine respect for all he had done for me and the ministry. I figured that even if it was wrong and difficult, it would be better to remain friends than be at odds.

Post Sail Media Production Company

Ironically, the same day that I received his call, the Voice of God spoke to me in a significant way.

I was riding in the back of a car with my executive assistant, Heather was in the front seat, and our good friend Ton was driving. We were moving at high speeds through the back alleyways of Rio De Janeiro and I became car sick. I planted my face into my suitcase positioned on my lap.

Enduring the motion and fighting to not get sick, I heard the Voice of God say to me, "I am giving you a post sail production."

I asked, "What is that?"

Looking at my assistant, I repeated exactly what the Lord had just spoken to me. S

he was used to me being a little eccentric anyhow, so she responded with, "Okay, Joseph," in a matter-of-fact, accepting tone. This is important to include because of the timeline of how everything unfolded. Years later, this word is still unfolding and has proved to be very true.

The Shift Begins

The "Cascade of Tragic Events" continued upon returning home from that trip overseas. One of the companies that had been supporting us financially came under scrutiny and was being investigated.

A number of people who attended our church also worked for this company, and Luke was one of two of the owners. He had worked for this company for many years, and when the opportunity to purchase half ownership arose, he mustered all he had to do so.

When the news of the investigation broke, it made the local papers. It was horrible for our church simply because it affected dear friends and church members. It was my desire to stand with all of the parties involved, even Luke.

Dave Duell Promoted to Heaven

Shortly after the news of this business scandal broke, we received the news that Dave Duell had fallen ill. Within a matter of days, he died. This was a crushing blow to many of us. Dave had asked me to take over his church in Denver. I had been reluctant because of all we had going on at the time. He was scheduled to speak at our upcoming fall conference, and I had been looking forward to spending time with him and talking through all the difficulties we had encountered.

His loss was unbelievable and unexpected. We were supposed to have many years together! Missing him was an understatement. Only a few months earlier, we had been ministering together in Brazil to thousands of people. He had been full of energy without any signs of weakness. Now we were saying goodbye.

Dave's funeral was surreal. So many people were there, and it felt wrong that he was actually gone. Something jumped inside of me at the end of Dave's life celebration, prompting to go see Andrew Wommack's Bible College in Woodland Park, CO. Yet, there was so much activity, I couldn't act on it at the time.

However, afterwards, a few of my team members went with me to the Charis Bible College campus, and we walked around the pond that faced Pike's Peak. The Holy Spirit said, "Remember this moment."

While there, I felt a strong sense of destiny and purpose. Shortly afterward, we met with the rest of our team in Woodland Park. As we were talking, they asked me if I thought we would all move to Colorado. It was strange, but even though I was stirred over Andrew Wommack's campus and ministry, my answer was, "No."

After attending Dave's home-going service, the world just didn't seem the same.

In addition, we had recently had a meeting with a few people, including Luke. I wanted to know what was up. Why was there an issue? Could we resolve it? He stonewalled me and said he knew things about me but didn't want to bring it out in that particular meeting. So, when I asked him privately what he meant by that, he had no information to share.

A day or so after we returned home from Colorado, my daughter and I decided to go for a ride on some small motorcycles a friend had given us. It seemed like a great way to get my mind off Dave's death, all that was happening with the ministry, and the impact of the business scenario.

We were flying around, laughing, but the pressure of everything was building in me. I was thinking about the team, who, in full trust, moved their entire lives to follow me, the ministry that was privately being shaken, and of course my friends who were now involved in this business issue. I was distracted.

Suddenly, while turning down a slope going too fast, the front wheel of the motor bike caught a root. The bike snapped to the left and out of my hands, launching me far down the path.

I was barely conscious when it dawned on me what had happened. My eyes were half open, and I was staggering back to the house when Ali caught up to me.

"Dad! Dad, are you okay? What's wrong?"

I recall hearing the sound of crunching in my back, neck, left shoulder, and all of my ribs. While walking and praying in tongues, I was thinking, *Get to the house... Pass out there... Heather will know what to do.*

When we came through the door, Heather got me to the couch and found that a part of the bike (likely the foot peg) had punched through my jeans and sliced into my shin, all the way to the bone. My back, shoulder, and rib cage were in agony.

The funny part of it all was that the pain was actually a relief from my thoughts of everything else that was going on. Later in the ER, they said it would have been better if I had broken all my ribs rather than sprain them to that degree.

Bad Pizza

Dave gone, busted up body, a number of my close friends under a legal investigation, and strange undercurrents within church leadership. This was the condition I was in right before our biggest annual fall conference, *Ignition*. I had serious thoughts of cancelling it, but out of principle, I decided against it.

On top of everything else, we were served legal papers regarding donations made to us by that business. My heart sank. Never having been in any kind of legal battle, I had no idea what it meant. We had to respond to the requests of the letter going right into our annual conference.

On top of that, while at the conference, there was Luke, sitting in the back row with all the now former leaders. I remember thinking, *Why are you even here?* Regardless, the sessions went on, and many people were blessed and ministered to. We soldiered up and served the people without any indication that there were issues at all.

The last day of the conference, fifty percent of the attendees became violently sick. It was serious. We never officially discovered the cause, but the pizza was the primary suspect. Ironically, to my knowledge, those who were sitting on the back row were not affected.

A Sad Revelation

About a year and a half later, Heather and I were brought in by the lead investigator for the state to interview us regarding the business scandal. One main purpose was to reclaim any donations made to the ministry. We decided to settle with them and pay back any questionable donations. It seemed to be the honorable thing to do, but also the wisest, since fighting it would have cost just as much.

After going through the interview, the lead investigator revealed to us why we had been brought in. He read to us a written accusation against us that we had been witnessed receiving a check for an enormous amount of money!

Heather and I looked at each other, then at the investigator, and asked, "Well, we have one bank. And, wouldn't you have found that in the business' records if that were the case?" All the puzzle pieces locked into place when he told us who had made this false accusation against us. It was none other than Luke.

Not long after that, Luke was discovered to have been in on some form of wrongdoing. Ultimately, he was sued for significantly more than the amount he had lied about us having. Sadly, the owner who had allowed him to buy half of his company was actually a good man who got played by both his former partner and Luke.

To this day, Luke's actions shock me. It's hard to understand why someone who was so respected by me and others would lie in such a dramatic way. I can only assume that it was to deflect from his own improper conduct.

The realization came to me about this. A good person who is outside of their designated lane, then empowered in that lane, can be pressured into doing wrong things.

Even so, we and those who were with us, prayed and decided to continuously bless and keep only sweet thoughts of him. We choose to focus on all the good times and we have no hard feelings toward one another. May the love and favor of God follow him the rest of his days!

The Return of Dear Friends

During this time, one of my oldest friends came back into my life. Adam and his wife, Kathy, were like a breath of fresh air in the midst of these difficult times. Two decades prior, I had worked for Adam as listing coordinator for one of his companies, and we had become great friends. They encouraged us through the entire process and were like the Voice of God in the middle of a storm.

Adam came from a challenging upbringing yet turned his life into a true rags-to-riches story. He took part in many successful business ventures, was in *Sports Illustrated* for powerlifting, and at one time owned one of the largest homes in the United States. Together, he and Kathy sowed millions of dollars into churches and missions, buying buildings for ministries around the world, among other things.

Their businesses and abilities were known around the world, all of which suffered both great challenges and rose to victory over the years. He would tell you today, the ups and downs of loss and success are not what define him.

Adam and I have had many laughs over pain and our refusal to let it crush us. He went through a vicious attack himself many years ago and has come full circle, becoming positioned on a global business stage. One of the things you discover about people of significance and substance is that they most often walk with a limp: they have a point of reference far different from those who always play it safe.

They know that life can cost a lot, but fundamentally believe risks are worth taking because nothing is worse than living "normal." Normal will not accomplish anything major. Adam and Kathy are, by definition, this type of people—my type of people! He is a walking book of proverbs, filled with inspirational wisdom. His perspective and wisdom of the journey is the value he imparts to everyone he meets. People from all over the world come to be mentored by and spoken into by the value he imparts.

One of my favorite things that Adam says is, "Some will. Some won't. So what?" Meaning, make the most of your journey and don't look at the shortcomings of others. Keep moving forward. And if you are blessed to have people come alongside you as you walk your path, that is a bonus!

It was encouraging when he said to me at the end of that difficult season, "You came from the palace to the manger, and your test has now become your testimony."

One of my favorite Kathy lines, in response to people who are judging you regarding your past challenges, "It concerns me that you don't have any past challenges. I know what I've stood through, but I don't know about you."

They spoke many such things into us during this transitional season. Thank you, Adam and Kathy! We are forever grateful for the relationship we have with you.

Twenty-Five Years Later

It had been a few months since those challenges we faced in Indiana. Adam and I were in Minneapolis for a special trip. On the morning of our last day there, Adam said he felt stirred by the Holy Spirit and shared a wonderful experience he had recently walked through with his father, who was also with us on this particular morning. Adam and his dad told me the moving story of their path to reconciliation. The two of them felt as if it was time for me to have restoration with my dad as well

It had been over twenty-five years since the night of my dad's fateful ultimatum. Adam and his father were loving on me and deeply wanted me to experience what they had. They were so earnest about this notion that they were even compelled to travel a few hours with me to see my dad. They believed that time had possibly made way for reconciliation.

The gesture was terrific, and after thinking it over with them, I decided to give the Lord the option to do something.

Besides, I lived states away, and it wasn't typical for my friend and his father to be in the same state as me at the same time. I decided it was worth a try, since it was a rare opportunity to do something significant with the support of two guys who had lived through something similar.

It was my honest desire to not let fear, or the past, rob me of something that could bring life. After agreeing to go, we began the nearly three-hour drive together. I realized that it was challenging for me to even bring an image of my dad's face to mind! It had been so many years since the last time I saw him.

When we finally arrived at our destination, we discovered that my dad was the principal of a school. Out of a desire to be kind and respectful, we waited until it was after hours, not wanting to cause any disruption.

Adam met with him first. He was gone for only a few minutes, but it seemed like an hour. As I waited in the car with his father, a wave of peace came over me. Thoughts of what they were talking about were rolling through my mind. Choosing to keep my emotions calm and my demeanor still was imperative to me. Then, Adam was back and quietly getting in the car.

Adam paused, "He doesn't want to meet with you, Joe." I was not surprised, but I was disappointed. Not sure how to respond, I just sat for a moment, processing what Adam had just said. He asked me, "Do you want to leave? Or what would you like to do?"

At this moment, my heart rose up and I responded, "Well, we didn't come this far to leave." Now, you really have to understand, my friend Adam is a bold man. I could tell that he was deeply hoping we would not leave with a whimper.

Once he knew I didn't want to leave, his boldness came through his response. "I think you should go in there."

It made me smile when I got out of the vehicle and noticed he was getting out as well. We looked at each other, then walked directly toward the front doors, and into the building.

I politely asked the front desk staff for permission to speak with him. They said, "Sure, he is in his office," gesturing the way.

When we approached the short hall, my eyes searched the space as we came around the wall leading up to the door of his office. He was leaning forward in his office chair, turned away from his desk, looking right at me as I walked in.

He was exactly the same, only twenty-five years older, his posture tolerating the moment.

"Hi, Dad."

He responded with, "Hi," immediately followed with a very terse, "What do you want?"

"Life is passing by. You have grandkids who would like to meet you. Can we at least communicate?" To my surprise, rather than warmth, his response was controlled rage.

I say controlled because it was clear he didn't want to make a scene with his staff nearby. For a moment, I was thirteen again. A little taken aback by his anger, I listened as he intensely painted me a picture.

"I have grandkids, but not your kids," He snapped. "I told you, I love you, and will always love you. And I told you that this day would come. I f****** told you."

Then he reminded me by adding, "You remember what I told you all those years ago? Just in case you forgot, let me remind you what I told you then, and promised I would tell you when this day came: f*** you... and please leave."

He dramatically pointed at the door, but went on to say, "I love you, and I have always loved you. However, it is because of my great love for you that I cannot have anything to do with you!"

I responded, "Do you hear yourself?" He broke in and said, "Now... please leave," again pointing at the door.

I exerted, "It doesn't have to be this way. Life is going by, and we are wasting time talking like this. We don't even have to agree!"

He interrupted me with that same controlled rage glaring at me, wanting to shout, but speaking as intensely as one can without doing so, "You made your choice!"

It was like time stood still as it all came back to me: my mom's broken jaw at his hand, and the surgery she needed to correct it, the verbal and physical abuse, the other things my siblings endured at this man's inexcusable behavior, and years of his rage and intimidation, among many other things.

The peace I walked in with was suddenly challenged as intense anger came over me in a way I had never experienced before. For a moment, I thought to myself, *I'm going to pummel this old man into the ground.* I had pictures running through my mind of the police showing up after I beat him to the floor for all he had done.

Then, in the same moment, I remembered the peace the Holy Spirit had given me in the car. This internal process took only a moment, but I concluded that the same peace was still available to me. It was as if the Voice of God said, "Don't take the bait. Show him love. He doesn't know what he is doing. Now, let that peace come over you again."

So, within a matter of seconds, I allowed that same peace to come over me, and I responded with, "I love you, and you were worth the attempt."

He said, "Okay, good, we understand each other... Now please leave." Again, pointing at the door. The conversation was exactly like it had been twenty-five years before. Only now, it was predicated on the statement, "I don't have a son, please leave."

I let go of any need for his approval and picked up my whole identity in Jesus. As I walked out of the office area, past his staff, I had the thought, *This could be the time to spice things up by going low and trashing him to them.*

But, when they asked how the meeting went, I responded, again being flooded by peace, "Great, he is a great guy."

They responded, "He is a great guy."

I said, "Thank you, ladies, for showing us in."

Adam stayed behind. It was only for a few moments, but it was long enough to let my dad know what a wasted opportunity it was for him and what he was missing out on. I didn't hear everything, but knowing Adam, I'm confident it made a lasting impression.

The conclusion with my dad is that I will always be available for true reconciliation. In my view, he is hurt and feels betrayed by nearly everyone. Pain is subjective, and his pain must be to the highest level in his own experience. I love him and bless him.

Thank you, Dad, for all you did for me as a kid. Thank you for teaching me to be strong. Thank you for a powerful work ethic. Some of the best parts of who I am are from you.

You Are Home

It was during this same season that Heather and I, along with Adam and Kathy, were on a trip to Colorado. We had been driving so much through the mountains that Heather and I didn't even know where we were. My friend, Jason, was driving. He and his wife, Stephanie, were among the top ten crop harvesters in the nation. They became very close friends during this seemingly endless season of transition.

We were all driving in a large SUV, up a long dirt road which lead directly to the base of a massive 14,000-foot mountain, when I heard the Voice of God say to me very clearly, like a command, "You will now go by the name Joseph Z."

It was so starkly clear in my heart that it was almost audible. I spoke out loud to everyone in the vehicle, "The Lord just told me that I am to go by the name Joseph Z!" Adam immediately responded with, "Now, *that* is a global name! That's a name that will go around the world."

Five minutes later, we came to the large entrance to our destination, and the Voice of God spoke to me again, "You are home."

I said out loud, "The Lord just told me I am home." This time no one answered. It was strange, saying that and not even knowing where we were! All I knew was that we were in Colorado somewhere, way out in the Rocky Mountains.

As we parked and got out of the vehicle, an English mastiff came running up to us. He was intimidating! The owner of the dog yelled, "Duke! Get back here!"

When I heard the name of my own childhood companion, it was surreal. In a matter of a few minutes, the Lord had given me a name change, told me I was home, and then I heard the name of my dog who had meant so much to me. The Spirit of the Lord said again, "You are home, now."

We soon discovered that this would, in fact, be our home. It would be a place to be hidden in the wilderness for a time to recover. To become strong again. Shortly after this encounter, we moved to Colorado, and for the next three years lived on a beautiful mountain. We affectionately call it Shiloh.

One day, while looking through an old photo album, I came across a picture of the time we had visited Dave Duell in Colorado. It was then that I realized that we had relocated to the exact mountain I had looked at every day while attending Dave's conference, when I had a revelation of Jesus and was commanded to preach the Complete Gospel. What an astonishing revelation! The Lord had moved us back to the same location of one of the most significant times in my life! It was like a surprise present hidden by God that took me months to put together.

During this season, a phrase became prevalent as we remained on the mountain. It was our time on the mountain that allowed us to transition from outcast into broadcast.

Thank You, Jesus.

Chapter Ten

Re-Sensitized to the Voice of God

The time of moving to Colorado and living isolated in the mountains was filled with restoration, as well as a repurposing for what mattered.

One of the things that happened was a pulling back from prophetic ministry. Why? Mostly because of seeing what happened to people during those sixteen years, coupled with the recent ministry challenges.

Over the years, experiencing people that either worship prophecy, or fight against it, turned the topic repulsive. It seemed as if there was no win for that type of ministry. Best to do away with it as much as possible and leave it to the enthusiastic.

After all, God certainly had better qualified, less dysfunctional people out there to flow in this style of ministry.

The Voice of God remained precious on a private level. However, my new goal was to go into business and teach the Bible on the side.

Have you ever heard the old joke, "If you want to make God laugh, tell Him your plans"? Yup, that about summed up my logic at that time.

However, there came a day of reckoning with the Holy Ghost. It wasn't harsh or negative, but it was overwhelming. This reckoning had two preceding encounters involving the Voice of God and an undeniable encounter with His presence. Interestingly, all three took place in a vehicle.

First Encounter

The first encounter settled the decision to marry Heather.

It happened during a time of questioning if we really wanted to get married. While I was driving alone (in the same minivan as the first time we met) on a Minneapolis highway, back in 1998, the Holy Spirit flooded my vehicle. It was so powerful—palpable. It was as if the Lord Himself had sat down in the passenger seat, and had I reached over, I could have physically touched Him!

However, an intense reverence and fear made it difficult to look, much less reach over, to the passenger seat. So, with eyes straight ahead and two hands on the wheel, time itself seemed to slow down. I felt like I was no longer driving but floating. Everything became silent, including the sounds of the road, wind and motor. It was like being in a vacuum.

A vision of Heather appeared. She was standing in a shaft of light, surrounded by unkind voices. I sensed that her life would be difficult if she wasn't with me, but that with me as a protector, she would reach her highest potential.

At the end of the vision, God asked, "Do you want Heather as your wife?"

Speechless for a moment, and unsure if this was some kind of test, my answer was, "Please, Sir, You decide."

It went quiet but the intense presence was still very apparent. After an awkward silence, I spoke up again, "You decide, but I sure do love Heather."

Suddenly, the presence lifted, and time and space returned to normal. Now completely aware of my surroundings, and curious how the van was still on the road, these words came out, "Did I do something wrong? Was that pleasing to you?"

Silence...

The next day was my birthday, so Heather came to where I was staying.

She said, "I've been thinking. Why are we wasting time trying to figure out if this is the right thing or not? I have an overwhelming sense that we should go forward!"

I responded, "Me too!"

There was never a question again. It was a long time before I told Heather about my encounter with God while driving down the highway.

Second Encounter

The second encounter was regarding Heather again.

One day, while she was in dialysis, I was sitting in the truck working and speaking out against the constant thoughts that Heather may die.

The doctors had consistently been telling us to prepare for the worst, as she had a variety of challenges throughout the whole process. Yet, she was a star patient due to overcoming odds; each time she received bad news, it was overturned with a miracle.

The Holy Spirit sustained her due to her intense daily routine of mixing her faith with the Word of God. She would spend hours every day listening to teaching that God wanted her healed and relentlessly meditating on scriptures. It got to the point that whenever we received bad news, we would start laughing in front of the doctors. They didn't know what to do with that. We would thank them and say, "It's not you. We just are expecting something far better!"

Even with these victories, the journey was still very taxing. Combating thoughts of her not making it, and having to raise our children without her, was a daily fight of faith. Yet, we knew that we were going to push forward.

It was a cold day while working out in that truck. The heater was on, and I was deep into my routine of answering emails, scheduling events, writing, media work, and the like. Suddenly, the atmosphere in the vehicle began to change, and that familiar, intense presence began to fill the truck.

Again, I was afraid to look at the passenger seat due to the intense palpable sensation engulfing me. This time, although the hair on my neck and arms was standing up, the presence of God wasn't there to present me with a choice. It was different. I felt a merciful and deeply loving sensation at the deepest level—beyond anything I had ever experienced before.

At first, silence was His vocabulary. I don't know how long the complete stillness lingered. It was impossible for me to say anything, as the presence was so overwhelming. Eventually, the Voice of God spoke clearly. It is difficult to say if it was audible or not, but one thing was sure—God spoke.

His Voice said, "I just want to look at you for a moment."

Now, bursting with tears and unable to speak, all I could do was listen intently. His unmistakable Voice spoke again, "You're doing a good job." A long pause followed, until He said, "You are going to be okay."

Tears were still rolling down my face as His presence lifted. It was a powerful moment—a direct promise from the Voice of God that everything was going to be okay, that we were following the right path.

As I came out of this moment, time and space once again returned to normal. Suddenly, it came to my attention that there were lights flashing behind me in front of the dialysis building. Quickly pulling myself together, I exited the truck and ran to the entrance to discover what was happening. My only thought was, *All that matters is that Heather is safe!*

A man who was seated not far from Heather in the unit decided that he no longer wanted to live. He began shouting, "I can't take this anymore!" and proceeded to pull the dialysis tubes out of his arm.

These tubes were connected to the main arteries that go to the heart, so when he ripped them out, his blood began spraying in every direction and onto the floor. It was horrible, as the power of his heart pumped his blood out, without any blockage.

The courageous nurses fought to rescue this man. Heather witnessed this in close proximity and was praying out loud, while also shouting along with the nurses, "Please stop! We don't want you to die!"

She had great compassion for him and the hopelessness he must have felt. The fire department and ambulance arrived with emergency lights and sirens blaring, in an attempt to save this man's life. We don't know if he lived or died, as he was rushed out of the facility and we never saw him again.

I still find it interesting that this encounter of the Lord's reassurance took place outside, just as this drama unfolded inside. Heather's powerful prayers and faith must have been a factor in this moment.

The Post Office Prophet

There were a number of prophetic moments leading up to our time in the mountains. For a number of years, it became almost routine!

The first one took place while walking into a post office to get the ministry mail and open a new post office box. While walking to the new box to test the keys, someone shouted at me, "Is your name Joseph?"

There were a good amount of people checking their mail also; it was a Minneapolis post office. After closing the box, turning toward the voice, my response was, "Yes!" The person calling my name was about sixty feet away, with several people between us.

The others quickly parted to the sides and exited the building. The man said, "The Lord would say to you, you are called to a new land and will go there. In this place, you will establish and build beyond those who trained you. The Lord has need of your voice and influence on a large scale, and you will leave many behind. This will be difficult for you, but necessary."

I thanked this post office prophet, and out of honor to the word of the Lord spoken through him, gave him all the cash that was in my wallet.

A Pot Blessing Prophecy

At the end of one of our evening church services, we had a potluck dinner, which we affectionately named "pot blessing". It was in typical church fashion, boasting paper plates, an assortment of veggies with dip, chips, coffee and chili. I was tired and had inner plans to pull back and fade out of the picture, partly because of Heather, and partly because of our intense schedule. There was no one to talk to about this without discouraging those around me.

This particular service, my associate pastor was speaking. When finished, we gathered downstairs. An African man abruptly walked up to within an arm's reach of me. I had never seen him before and haven't seen him since. Stuck in a corner with a paper plate in hand, there was no route of escape. It all seemed very unusual.

He said, "The Lord sent me here to tell you something! You cannot quit now! The Lord has need of you and your written words! You have a message that the Lord has given you that must go across America!" I knew that he was talking about when the Holy Spirit told me to preach to the masses with the Complete Gospel.

"You have thought about slowing down and stepping out of sight, and you must not! God has called you and not another! Are not His prophet?! You are called to prophesy the Word of God! Bless you, Man of God." Then he left just as abruptly as he had come. No one knew who he was.

Police Officer Prophecy

We were staying at the home of our friends John and Eunice, way up in the cold reaches of northern Minnesota. The Holy Spirit told me to go to a certain man's house because this particular man had a word for me. It was not far away; it was within walking distance. After walking and praying for a bit, about what the Holy Spirit had spoken, my feet found the front doorstep of this man's home. After sheepishly knocking on the door with no answer, I decided that he was most likely not home.

As I left the porch, there was a sense of leaving something uncompleted; I had no feeling of closure. I didn't understand why the Holy Spirit would speak to me about receiving a word from a specific person, but the person was not home.

After returning to John and Eunice's house, I set out on the three-hour journey back to Minneapolis. It was a long drive home that evening. That experience caused an unresolved question mark for many years.

Fast forward fifteen years: I was speaking at a church in that same area. The meetings were good, and people were blessed. The last night, as we were on our way back to the hotel, my friend Jason was driving, and Heather was in the back seat making us all laugh. This was a typical scenario while driving after a meeting. Suddenly, lights were flashing behind us; a squad car was pulling us over!

The officer came to the window and explained that although we were slightly speeding, he was mostly pulling us over because he hadn't seen anyone on the road all night. (I'm not saying that Jason was driving slowly. This is "GIT-R-DONE—JASON, THE HARVEST MASTER we're talking about.)

The officer was kind and humorous. In the course of our conversation, we told him we had been speaking at a local church. This is where it gets interesting. Accompanying the officer was a chaplain. As we continued talking, the officer was abruptly moved out of the way by this chaplain! All at once, he leaned through the window, across Jason, grabbed me by the arm, and declared, "THE LORD SAYS TO YOU…" I thought, *Whoa, what's happening?!* But this chaplain prophesied over me!

Shockingly, he prophesied in detail about specifics regarding the last season of our journey, about many things from the last two years when we experienced isolation and recovery. He spoke about our challenges and how we had survived and overcome them. Then he went on to declare what was coming next.

He said, "There is a SHIFT HAPPENING RIGHT NOW for you, and more will come out of you than ever before! You are not done with the areas you are ministering in, and there will be more fruit than ever! There is a new city God is calling you to, and there will be a type of center, or meeting hub, that will begin to train and produce leaders and prophetic voices. Music will come out of it as well." Many more accurate and powerful things were spoken over us.

Tears gushed down my face, knowing the Lord was powerfully speaking.

Part of the overflow of emotion was the sudden realization that this chaplain was the same man whose house the Holy Spirit had sent me to for a word, fifteen years before.

The Voice of God whispered to me, "Delay is not denial." The word meant so much more following a fifteen year wait. It made the whole process special and showed me that the Lord knew what we were going to go through fifteen years beforehand!

How awesome is that?!

The Sign to Establish

On a fall day, while on a ministry trip to the state of Washington, I was alone in a hotel room when the Voice of God spoke. During a time of prayer and seeking Him early in the morning, suddenly He said, "Get up and go downstairs to the restaurant."

"Yes, Sir." I got up and headed out the door. It seemed strange, but it has become clear to not question when I know it is the Voice of God. Upon stepping out of the elevator and walking into the dining area, Jason was there. Joining him and surveying the room, my eyes locked onto someone familiar. It was Brian Head Welch, the lead guitarist from the rock band Korn. This was a thrill because Brian and I had done a conference together a few years prior.

Immediately, I got up and walked over to introduce myself to Brian and his daughter. He said, "Minneapolis, right?" I said, "That's right!" Followed with, "Good to see you." The Voice of God prompted me to give him all the money I had. So that's exactly what I did. He was grateful and blessed me for it. We hugged and both hoped to see each other again.

Just before leaving, out of my mouth came, "I'm going to be ministering with Todd White soon." On the inside, I said to myself, *Why would you say something like that?!* Todd White is a global evangelist who touches masses of people all over the world with the love of God, and often displays miracles. At the time I didn't even know Todd, and certainly hadn't been scheduled to speak with him.

Brian said, "That's awesome! Say hi to him for me!"

Leaving with an internal question mark directed at myself, I again asked, *Why in the world would you say something like that!?* The Voice of God rose up inside saying, "I prompted those words, not you."

When I returned to my room, I hit my knees to pray. He went on to say, "Establish in Colorado. You will now begin to minister in different circles and go up the ladder to a different level of influence."

"Yes, Sir."

Nine months later, I was ministering in Brazil with Todd White.

Grocery Store Prophet

In this same season, Heather was prompted to go to the grocery store, and my mom and I both came along. A man approached us in the parking lot because he liked my truck. My truck was pretty impressive: black with oversized tires. I understood his interest because it was an awesome truck!

While talking, it seemed as though we couldn't break away. He kept talking and talking. It seemed as though the Holy Spirit was leading us to keep listening to him, so we did. After a long time, the internal conversation inside me became more persistent. *Why am I still listening to this man go on and on? Why am I making Heather and my mom listen to this too?* We even had friends come up to greet us, who eventually just left. Still, I had no peace to leave.

Suddenly, a voice broke the conversation. It was a dear friend of ours from Missouri, Glenda! She hugged and loved on us! It messed with me a little bit because Glenda is also a proven prophet of God. My internal dialogue went from wondering, *Why?* to, *Uh oh... God sent a prophet to speak to me! He wanted us to wait here so that we didn't miss Glenda!*

After talking to us and loving on us, Glenda looked at me as only a prophet can. She paused and said, "Huh. You're hiding. It's time for you to step back into your call."

It was true! I *was* hiding! The years after moving to the mountain was a time where the desire to minister had become very dim. The prophetic had simply lost its appeal.

However, this moment jarred me.

Prophecy from India

One day, I received a text message from a friend describing a peculiar conversation he and another friend had with a man from India during a business call. Somehow, their topic of conversation changed, and my name was mentioned. The moment this man heard my name, he stopped the conversation and prophesied about me! Not knowing me, or anything about me, this man was overtaken by the Holy Spirit and spoke what he saw regarding me.

Word for word, the message read:

"You'll be planting a lot of churches, but they are not normal churches.

"These are churches that the HG [Holy Ghost] will come and do whatever He wants.

"You are going to be an apostle over these churches and will administrate them all.

"These churches will not only be in the US but all over the world.

"One thing. I saw a square piece of flesh and the dragon is trying to squeeze the flesh. The devil is trying to squeeze something from your past. The devil has been working on

that. God is going to bring total healing before you put on the whole armor of God."

The presence of the Lord came on me strongly when I read this. I knew God was setting me up to become completely strengthened after the challenges we had faced in life and ministry. This was the piece of flesh that would become healed before the armor would go back on. Shortly after this came my third encounter.

Third Encounter

The two previous encounters with the presence of the Lord came with great power and a tangible sense that He was physically present with me. Each time, those encounters took place in a vehicle, and this was no different.

While sitting in my truck, I began to watch a video of an inspiring Bible teaching someone had sent to me. After listening for nearly an hour, the teaching portion of the message came to an end. The minister in the video stepped out into the large audience to pray and prophesy.

In this moment, that familiar, palpable sense of the presence of the Lord filled the vehicle. There was an even more intense reverence and fear this time than at the other times. It was so powerful that I was unable to muster the ability to speak.

He said, "You know what I have called you to do." Still unable to speak, intense tears flooded my face.

The question came, "Will you do it? Will you minister to the people?"

This may sound odd to you as you read this (I know it would to me if I hadn't actually experienced it), but a breaking began to happen inside of me. I was still unable to speak as the weight and intensity of His presence was almost suffocating. It wasn't terrifying, it was just intensely serious regarding the call on my life, and my heart was flooded with love and passion as He spoke to me.

Finally, I rallied the strength to verbally answer, "YES! LORD, YOU ARE MY GOD! I WILL DO IT! I LOVE YOU!"

From that point on, as crazy and embarrassing as this sounds, all I could do was scream. Whenever my mouth opened to speak, it would come out as a scream.

Finally, the pain induced apathy toward my calling was broken off. His presence was loving but serious about what He required of me. Yet, the choice was mine. It wasn't like He was giving me an ultimatum, as though if I didn't do this, I would miss my whole destiny. Instead, I felt a sense of proper timing and that it was now my moment to step forward again and leave my rejection of prophecy behind.

It had never been my intention to despise it, but somewhere along the sometimes-painful journey, I had allowed my heart to grow hard in that area. In this moment, the love and power of God shattered that hardness to pieces.

Not long after this, our friends insisted on us attending Andrew Wommack's Ministers' Conference in Woodland Park, Colorado. As you will read in the pages ahead, it rocked me back into the game.

The season of being an outcast had truly come to a close. Now it was time to broadcast!

Chapter Eleven

Sowing into the Future

At the end of one of the sessions of Andrew Wommack's Ministers' Conference, Heather and I remained seated in the auditorium. Altar ministry was still happening, but fellowship was dwindling around the room.

A friend of ours from Minnesota, who had attended meetings of ours in the past, approached us and said, "I need you to meet someone." He introduced us to a man who held many responsibilities at Charis Bible College and Andrew Wommack Ministries.

I recognized the man, and as I reached out my hand to shake his, I said, "We have already met at Dave Duell's funeral."

With obvious emotion touching his voice, he replied, "You knew Dave?"

"Yes," I answered. "He meant a lot to me. We traveled and ministered together a great deal the last few years of his life."

We had an instant connection; something came alive in both of us. It seemed as if we had known each other our entire lives!

Suddenly, the words "social security" appeared across the chest of my new friend. My eyes filled with tears as the Voice of God spoke to me, "Today, you will be this man's social security."

I said to him, "Stay here, please, and don't leave; I will be right back!" While gesturing to Heather to please wait with him, I ran as fast as possible to our vehicle. There were a few thousand dollars we had brought along to sow into ministry. The Voice of God spoke again, saying, "All of that."

I hastily returned to the meeting, and, with great humility, placed several thousand dollars into the hands of the man of God!

A Symbolic Seed

This meeting turned into a relationship that began to further alter the direction of my heart. It wasn't long after, while looking at my custom, black pickup truck, that the Lord offered me a choice. "If you are willing, I have need of your vehicle for him." This truck had great meaning because it was the first major vehicle breakthrough we had ever experienced.

A prophet had come to me a few years prior saying, "You have sown seed, and the Lord is pleased. It will be a sign unto you that you will be given two cars at the same time." My thought at that moment was, *Amen. Received in Jesus' Name!* Then I sort of forgot about it.

That is, until roughly six months later, after supernaturally raising money to buy a pastor a brand-new truck, someone approached me saying they wanted to give me a new car. We were thrilled and graciously received it! That same weekend, another person who owned an auto dealership was meeting with us, and another brother stood up saying, "I believe God just said Joseph is supposed to receive a new truck today!"

The dealer replied, "Okay, let's do it!" Within one weekend, Heather received a car and I was given my custom, black truck. The word came to pass. Until this time, we had only owned much older cars. This was a monumental breakthrough. Not only was the truck amazing to look at, with many custom features such as large tires, it had most of the modern amenities available at the time. It was a symbol that our days of poverty were over. Giving radically worked!

When God's request came, there was a slight hesitation, not because of how nice the vehicle was, but simply what it represented to me. However, ultimately my answer was, "Yes." Upon that simple word to the Lord, I burst into tears and the powerful sense of the changing of a season rose up within. The Holy Spirit was so tangible as that symbolic truck was joyfully sowed.

God's Economy

This became a season of sowing into our future. God's economy of sowing and reaping is so much more powerful than any system mankind has. So, Heather also decided to sow her car into another ministry, a couple who were developing a national itinerant youth conference.

Heather and I both felt compelled that if we were going to step into the highest calling God had for us, then it was very important that we sow our way into that season. We decided, *If we are going to move forward, it's time to radically sow into the future!*

At every event and ministry-related scenario in which we found ourselves, we decided we would financially give as much as we could possibly give. In addition to giving away our vehicles, we would walk up and sow directly into leaders who were already on television and operating on large media platforms. Our purpose was to sow where we were headed.

After joyfully sowing a total of six vehicles and completely depleting any and all the resources we possessed, we thanked God that our future was in His hands. There is a great liberty in trusting Him with all you have! This induced the opening of many supernatural doors to us. We know that it was the hand of God because only He would have been able to cause us to have so much favor.

However, this was the exchange: we gave all we had, and He did the rest. It's like the old saying we often use, "If you do the difficult, God will do the impossible!" **It takes sowing into your future to have something waiting on you when you arrive there.** That is exactly what happened to us regarding entering our new season.

The sowing of seed has always been a major part of our lives. It was previously the avenue that broke us out of debt, and it became the avenue which opened the doors into that fresh arena and new season.

This is hilarious for someone like me, who at the age of eighteen, when first exposed to the idea of giving large amounts of money, considered it preposterous! I thought that it must be only for those who have a special gift of giving. Even when a friend once gave three hundred dollars in a church service, it seemed like an impossible thing to me.

Poverty thinking surrounded us, even after Heather and I were married. We only knew lack. We lived in a small cabin in the woods. The living room, bedroom and kitchen were all one room, with a closet-sized bathroom possessing the only door inside the little place. Things were so tight that I would sometimes hunt grouse so we could eat.

We started listening to messages that taught us that God wanted us to prosper. It was challenging to our poverty belief system. Yet, it opened a door of faith enough that the first time the Lord spoke to us as a married couple to sow a car, we actually did it! We sowed our car and shortly after were given a much nicer car out of the blue!

Even with the understanding of God's economy as it relates to giving, it wasn't until this season that we began walking in a much higher level on the receiving end. If you have never sown aggressively, I recommend it!

If you have a desire to hear the Voice of God with more clarity, a generous heart will make His voice much clearer. Remember, you are only giving into your future! God's economy is activated by trust in Him and that trust is shown by giving.

Go for it, because your future life will benefit from the favor God wants to show you that can only be accessed through giving. We have become bold when talking about God's economy because we aggressively live it. Someone once said, "Generous giving can become addicting, and God will support your habit!"

Significant Relationships

There were so many people who got upset after they found out what had taken place between my dad and I when Adam and I went to see him. It became uncomfortable to talk about because it seemed that those who heard the story were far more troubled by it than I was.

Over the years, a number of wonderful people had offered to fill this missing role of a father in my life. However, most often, it was not a fit. Resolve had set in my heart with the thought, *If I can't have a father, then I will be the best one I know how to be.*

Yet, at this point, significant figures began to step into our lives, many of whom came through Andrew Wommack's ministry. It sparked a time of restoration in a way we hadn't thought was possible. Yet, it was happening.

Steak Knife into a Butter Knife

This season was a complete recalibration of the gift and calling on my life, a time of becoming usable in the hands of God as He tenderized me through love, and defining the true purpose of what it means to minister to people. One friend likened the process to going from a steak knife to a butter knife. Rather than an instrument used for cutting, the function would now be spreading the love of God through His Word.

A gift can either be wielded as a steak knife or a butter knife, depending on what belief system has honed it! This made all the difference: realizing that ministry isn't about building a platform and working hard, being driven by ambition. What a lesson. How easy it is to mistake ambition for calling! The difference is revealed through a revelation of the finished works of Jesus, as we will discover in the upcoming pages.

I still laugh to myself regarding what I am about to write. Because it was through this season of restoration and Holy Spirit healing that one day it dawned on me: **ministry is about people!** That's right, it isn't about expanding influence or building platforms. Those things are simply a byproduct of loving people.

A better way of saying it is, "Ministry is letting Jesus love people through us." It sounds simple, but it became a clear revelation because of our season of separation. Loving people was my transition from a steak knife into a butter knife.

The Voice of God

A new chapter in our lives had begun to be penned with an eloquence I had never experienced before. It was the Voice of God that led my family onto the clearest path we had ever walked. Knowing Jesus and His Voice is the most significant way to live.

Chapter Twelve

Jesus Is the Voice of God

All my experiences and journeys through hearing the Voice of God have led me to one conclusion: Jesus is the Voice of God. When we realize the Holy Spirit is that extension of Jesus Who speaks, it reveals a life-giving perspective on how God communicates.

> *"My sheep hear My voice, and I know them, and they follow Me."*
>
> – John 10:27

Jesus and the Word of God Are Synonymous

Jesus and the Word of God are synonymous. This is a powerful understanding when it begins to completely sink in, giving you a whole new perspective on the Word of God. Your approach, your study and how you hear His Voice will all develop with much more clarity and potency when you realize that the Word of God is Jesus speaking to you.

The level of your appreciation of the inspired Word is a measuring stick that will reveal how accurately you are hearing Him.

God Has Spoken to Us by His Son

"God, who at various times and in various ways spoke in time past to the fathers by the prophets, [2] has in these last days spoken to us by His Son, whom He has appointed heir of all things, through whom also He made the worlds; [3] who being the brightness of His glory and the express image of His person, and upholding all things by the word of His power, when He had by Himself purged our sins, sat down at the right hand of the Majesty on high."

– Hebrews 1:1-3

God is always speaking. The question is, are you listening? In Hebrews 1:1, notice it says that God spoke in various times and in various ways. In the past tense, it says He spoke through the prophets to the fathers. Then, using the present tense, it says that in ***these*** last days, He has spoken to us by His Son, Jesus.

It is a fascinating point the writer makes at the end of verse 2 when he says, "through whom also He made the worlds." God made everything we see through Jesus! Jesus is the Word of God and God spoke things into being by utilizing His Voice—Jesus!

This is reinforced in Proverbs 8 where most scholars agree that it is a preincarnate Jesus speaking and talking about how the world was formed.

"The LORD possessed me at the beginning of His way, Before His works of old. ²³ I have been established from everlasting, from the beginning, before there was ever an earth. ²⁴ When there were no depths I was brought forth, when there were no fountains abounding with water. ²⁵ Before the mountains were settled, before the hills, I was brought forth; ²⁶ While as yet He had not made the earth or the fields, or the primal dust of the world. ²⁷ When He prepared the heavens, I was there, When He drew a circle on the face of the deep, ²⁸ When He established the clouds above, When He strengthened the fountains of the deep, ²⁹ When He assigned to the sea its limit, So that the waters would not transgress His command, When He marked out the foundations of the earth, ³⁰ Then I was beside Him as a master craftsman; And I was daily His delight, Rejoicing always before Him, ³¹ Rejoicing in His inhabited world, And my delight was with the sons of men."

– Proverbs 8:22-31

Master Craftsman — A masculine noun meaning architect or craftsman. The word is used in Proverbs 8:30 as the personification of wisdom. Wisdom is portrayed as a craftsman at God's side, involved in designing the creation.

Proverbs 8:25 reads, "I was brought forth." This is a glimpse of when the Lord God almighty looked into darkness and declared, "Let there be light!"

"And God said, 'Let there be light,' and there was light."

– Genesis 1:3

In the above verse, pay attention to the use of the words "God said". What He spoke with was His own words, or the Word made flesh that God the Father brought forth to unleash onto the darkness and create the light and the world to follow. The Word He brought forth, or possessed at the beginning, was Jesus! Jesus is the Voice of God!

Jesus Holds All Creation Together!

All things are held together by the Word of His power. This means that God cannot break His Word! If He ever went back on one of His words, the whole universe would unravel at the molecular level!

> *"Who being the brightness of His glory and the express image of His person, and upholding all things by the word of His power, when He had by Himself purged our sins, sat down at the right hand of the Majesty on high."*

> *– Hebrews 1:3*

> *"He is before all things, and in him all things hold together."*

> *– Colossians 1:17, NIV*

He gave Jesus the name above all names.

> *"I will worship toward Your holy temple, And praise Your name For Your lovingkindness and Your truth; For You have magnified Your word above all Your name."*

> *– Psalm 138:2*

You Are a Voice of God!

Jesus is also the Word made flesh according to John Chapter 1. This world was formed by words, or *the* Word of God—Jesus. This is the very reason this world responds to words, especially the words of Jesus. When you, as a voice in this world, begin to speak the words of Jesus in faith, you also are operating as a Voice of God.

The Tone of God's Voice

You can see the tone by which God speaks also displayed in the persona of Jesus. This point is given greater clarity by the response Jesus gave to Philip when Philip asked Jesus to "show us the Father."

> *"Philip said to Him, 'Lord, show us the Father, and it is sufficient for us.' [9] Jesus said to him, 'Have I been with you so long, and yet you have not known Me, Philip? He who has seen Me has seen the Father; so how can you say, "Show us the Father?"'"*

– John 14:8-9

The tone of God's voice is displayed in the life of His son. Jesus never made anyone sick, nor did He ever curse anyone to death. Jesus boldly declared, "I have come to give you life and life more abundantly. It is the devil who comes to steal, kill, and destroy."

> *"The thief cometh not, but for to steal, and to kill, and to destroy: I am come that they might have life, and that they might have it more abundantly."*

– John 10:10, KJV

Remember this statement every time you wonder what God is really like. Jesus is the Voice of God, and the Father's tone is displayed through the life of the Son!

Do Not Go Beyond What Is Written

This is why when dealing with experiences and prophetic encounters, it is vital to hold fast to the Word of God! In 1 Corinthians 4:6, Paul stated, "Learn from us to not go beyond what is written." What a statement!

The Corinthians were a wild group of people. They were very carnal, sinful and had behavior issues that wandered far outside the lines of what even ungodly people would consider immoral. In addition, strange as it may sound, they were also highly spiritual!

What a combination: immoral and highly spiritual at the same time. This is why Paul's admonition is important, especially for anyone experiencing or stepping into a higher level of supernatural encounters. "Learn from us to not go beyond what is written." Sadly, this is true today in some circles within the Body of Christ. Often times, people who are consumed with hearing God and experientialism have little regard for the standard of truth laid out in the Word of God. The purest form of hearing God's Voice is through His written Word.

We Must Use the Word of God As Our Measuring Stick or We Are Out of Order

One day, a young man sitting in front of me told me about all his supernatural encounters, visions, dreams, and fantastic experiences. It was truly fascinating to listen to. At one point, however, it dawned on me : as he was speaking, not one reference to the Word of God was made.

After listening a while longer, I asked the question, "Have you been reading the Bible to make sure your experiences are in balance with the ultimate authority of God's Word?"

The young man looked bewildered by such a question. He said, "Well, when I was younger, I read the Bible all the time, and today, I just don't see a use for it."

I graciously responded, "Then your experiences are not valid to me." This didn't please him! I went on to say, "If you do not place your experiences and encounters under the authority of the Word of God, all you have left is your own process. You are left to your own emotional understanding and limited points of view. You will become weird, at the very least, and even completely deceived, if you do not incorporate the Word of God into your mind and heart."

His body language and composure conveyed that he did not like what he was hearing. He seemed put off by the idea that his experiences weren't valid without being under the authority of the Word of God. This was a somewhat shocking response to me because it has always seemed like common sense to have the Word of God be the guiding factor for the supernatural. Sadly, the process this young man conveyed is becoming more and more the way many are having a relationship with the Voice of God.

No Word, No Measuring Stick

Without the Word of God, you can fall for anything. Before we were done speaking that day, I told the young man his experiences weren't special and that I've had many similar, and so have countless other individuals over the years. What he failed to recognize was that without the written Word of God as the guideline for our encounters, all experiences can be subjective. It can actually become a delusion. The Word of God will ultimately empower healthy experiences and give people the staying power to master their experiences, rather than the other way around.

When someone does not place value on the Word of God, they do not place real value on Jesus. Jesus even said, "Why do you call me Lord, but not do what I tell you?"

> *"And why call ye me, Lord, Lord, and do not the things which I say? [47] Whosoever cometh to me, and heareth my sayings, and doeth them, I will shew you to whom he is like: [48] He is like a man which built an house, and digged deep, and laid the foundation on a rock: and when the flood arose, the stream beat vehemently upon that house, and could not shake it: for it was founded upon a rock. [49] But he that heareth, and doeth not, is like a man that without a foundation built an house upon the earth; against which the stream did beat vehemently, and immediately it fell; and the ruin of that house was great."*
>
> – Luke 6:46-49, KJV

Many people want the emotional encounter of calling Jesus, "Lord," worshiping Him, touching Him emotionally and having spiritual experiences. However, it is an entirely different level of commitment when we do what He says. The only way we can do what He says is to read what He says and value it!

The Testimony of Jesus Is the Spirit of Prophecy

The inspired Word of God is the testimony of Jesus. This is the same spirit by which prophecy works. **Prophecy, or things we discern as God's voice, are not equal to Scripture.** Although, we hear and experience the Voice of God in the same way the Scripture was written—through the inspiration of the Holy Spirit—this does not mean we can place the same value on a prophetic encounter as we place on Scripture.

The process and means by which we hear are the same, but nothing is equal to the Word of God in authority. The canon is closed and will never be added to. All prophecy is meant to confirm scriptural truth and principles. If it does not, it is to be disposed of without question.

> *"And I fell at his feet to worship him. But he said to me, 'See that you do not do that! I am your fellow servant, and of your brethren who have the testimony of Jesus. Worship God! For the testimony of Jesus is the spirit of prophecy.*[4] *'"*

> – Revelation 19:10

The testimony of Jesus is declared when the Holy Spirit uses prophetic voices in the body of Christ.

Jesus said, "I do not testify of myself, but my testimony comes from my Father" (John 5:31-37). Jesus' testimony is by the Holy Spirit through the inspired Word of God. This is also the reason we say, "If anything we encounter prophetically does not line up with the Word of God, then we should throw it away."

---

[4] I strongly encourage you to research the Greek words for "testimony", "spirit", and "prophecy".

It is of the utmost importance to always hold fast to the truth that the glory of Jesus is the aim of all prophecy. Why? Because He is the Word made flesh. He is the Word of God. Jesus is the Voice of God manifested in the Holy Spirit (the Spirit of Jesus). That is the driving point made by the angel in Revelation 19:10.

The angel had an instant reaction when John fell down to worship him. "See that you do not do that!" It feels almost frantic, as if this angel already witnessed what happened to lucifer when he wanted the worship God received. "Please don't worship me! Worship God! For the testimony of Jesus is the spirit of prophecy."

If we look deeper at what is being conveyed, we can also see that prophecy is clearly meant to be a testimony about Jesus: to cause anyone on the receiving end of prophetic activity to be influenced by the testimony of Jesus. We see this same truth made in 1 John 5:10. Prophecy should always line up with the witness of God through the Son Jesus Christ.

> *"He who believes in the Son of God has the witness in himself; he who does not believe God has made Him a liar, because he has not believed the testimony that God has given of His Son."*

> – 1 John 5:10

Colossians 2:18 mentions those who intrude into those things which they have not seen. It is highly important in the discussion of the prophetic that we continue to give the Lord glory, and this is another reminder to not go beyond what is written.

> *"Let no man beguile you of your reward in a voluntary humility and worshipping of angels, intruding into those things which he hath not seen, vainly puffed up by his fleshly mind."*

> – Colossians 2:18, KJV

Bringing Order to Encounters

If you recognize that spending time in the Word of God, and mixing it with your faith, is spending time with Jesus, this will bring proper identification of supernatural encounters. Having the Word of God as our foundation is mandatory for leading into spiritual gifts, and most critical when we define the Voice of God. In our church culture, there is a spiritual confusion that is wildly rampant.

Today, if someone has a supernatural experience, they are most often left to their own superstition, logic or religious point of view to figure it out. This is a recipe for deception and disaster, which is what I want to avoid by writing this.

Those who are experiencing supernatural things and do not have a guidepost, or a standard by which to measure truth and falsehood, are on a fast track to becoming deceived and unstable. Just because something is supernatural doesn't mean it should be legitimized as good.

Many people I have dealt with over the years have opened up to me about encounters they have experienced. A good number of these, oftentimes, turn out to be nothing more than circumstantial; or worse, the babbling of an unstable mind.

I certainly do not pretend to be an authority on the psychology of why people experience some "fantastic" things that are likely off-base, while others experience things that are genuine. This whole thing has always been a delicate topic as there are so many unbalanced people who either want to be legitimized by some wild experience, or their elevator is busted and doesn't quite go to the top floor.

This doesn't concern only unstable people but also religious spheres that instigate a supernatural hysteria, causing many well-intending people to be engulfed in an atmosphere that flaunts its ignorance by allowing anything and everything to happen under the label of the Holy Spirit.

The conclusions I have arrived at are based on the Word of God, and ultimately give us the proper tools for the answers we are looking for. I often say, "The best form of deliverance is ongoing, good teaching!" In this context, the best form of rightly dividing the weird from the legitimate is ongoing, good teaching!

Every person has thoughts, impressions and emotions. Every single day, we carry out the act of thinking to ourselves. This goes from minor to major. *What should I wear today? Traffic is slow. That TV show was funny.* All the way to thoughts about death, loved ones, arguments, money and so much more. These thoughts each create an emotional reaction.

However, impressions are based on a sense of an un-induced awareness. Oftentimes, impressions are derived from moments with people or engaged by your five senses. You may smell something and it makes a situational impression on you based off of a memory with a similar smell. Impressions can also rise up from a deeper place. This deeper place is actually the start of discovering the spiritual gifts.

These thoughts, impressions and emotions are a form of voice. They may not use spoken words, but they definitely communicate to you. It is vital to understand that any voice originates from one of two sources: God or the devil. It really is that simple. You are either entertaining God or the devil through what you allow to flow through your heart and mind.

If you are neutral, daydreaming often, with very little checks and balances confronting your thoughts to bring them in order by the Word of God, then you are very open to the wrong voice. What you are listening to, more of that will be

152

given to you. What you are thinking about is where you are headed. What you are looking at will ultimately manifest in your heart, mind and, ultimately, actions. The priority of managing what voice you are allowing to influence you is paramount to either living a life of liberty or bondage to feelings and emotions.

Manifestations of God's voice have come in a variety of ways. He has spoken through burning bushes, in a still small voice, etc. There is a term called a theophany. This is a theological term meaning an appearance of God in visible, temporary form and not necessarily material.

Before Jesus was manifested, God often spoke through theophanies. He is still highly capable of doing so in this New Testament time in which we live. The difference today is that we have new, regenerated spirits made one with Jesus, by which we cry out, "Abba, Father!" This means that today, when God speaks to us through His Son by the Holy Spirit, it is a local call!

God Is Always Speaking

It is liberating to know that God is **always** speaking. He is speaking to you all the time. Whether you know this or not, God wants to speak to you more than you want to hear Him! This is true! He made a way for all of us who are in Jesus to hear Him without the need for a priest, a prophet, or anyone. He made it so we can have one-on-one, direct communication with Him!

When you understand how true access to the realm of the spirit works, you will also discover that the devil is a legalist. He is in the spiritual realm, so he needs the cooperation of an individual who lives in this natural realm to gain access to their life and actions. He is a roaring lion seeking whom he may devour.

"Be sober, be vigilant; because your adversary the devil walks about like a roaring lion, seeking whom he may devour. ⁹ Resist him, steadfast in the faith, knowing that the same sufferings are experienced by your brotherhood in the world."

– 1 Peter 5:8-9

This verse is so revealing. Notice the devil roars and seeks whom he may devour. He cannot just jump out of the forest and attack and eat someone! He has only one weapon: his voice! He roars, or speaks, by making suggestions and putting thoughts into your mind. You will give the devil access to devour various areas of your life if you do not resist the thoughts and suggestions he sends to you.

The Devil's Native Language Is Lying

Remember Eve in the garden? The serpent spoke to her. She wasn't shocked that it spoke because she was in an environment that was both natural and supernatural. The supernatural was normal.

This is one reason I believe she engaged in conversation with it. After all, Eve had been accustomed to hearing the Lord God speak with Adam in the cool of the day. When this serpent spoke, she heard it.

It is not wrong to hear something. Eve's mistake was that she listened and reasoned with it. Imagine what would have happened if Eve responded to the serpent by saying, "I don't know you. I don't recognize your voice. Let me go see what the Lord has to say about this."

She could have dismissed the serpent by saying, "No," and gone to the Voice she knew. If she had, it is possible we would all be in a very different scenario today.

Through the devil's persuasion, Eve and Adam chose to believe his voice over God's. I say they chose because Eve was deceived, but not Adam. He knew very well what he was doing (Timothy 2:14; Genesis 3:6).[i]

Think about it. Because of that serpent's voice, Adam and Eve chose to agree with what was said. In doing so, they handed over their God-given authority, giving the devil dominion on this earth.

Here Is Some Really Good News

The voice of the devil is easy to defeat if you understand what to do! You need to know that he is defeated and the BIGGEST LOSER IN THE HISTORY OF CREATION. He is a deceiver; that is the only way he has any authority!

The counterfeit voice of darkness, the devil, is the ultimate counterfeit of the Voice of God. He appears as an angel of light in the form of worldly, carnal knowledge that darkens the heart.

He attempts to pervert the principle of God's voice coming alive in you through His Word. He knows that if what you are hearing is opposed to the Word of God, and you meditate on it, then it becomes what you speak and act on in this physical world.

The world around us responds to words because it was created by words. The devil operates through the power of suggestion. The fiery darts of the enemy are thoughts looking for a place to take root. The talking snake in the garden was all a perversion of the Voice of God.

It is the same today. The devil wants your meditation and words to reflect his delusional belief system. This will keep blessing from being realized and give power to the curse.

As an angel of light, he represents a supernatural knowledge, or special knowledge that is actually earthly, carnal and demonic. What you think about is where your life is headed. The kingdom of darkness knows this, and it is the only weapon they have to influence you and society. This is why the Word of God is vital to hearing accurately and standing against the wiles, or mind games, of the devil.

However, we are living under a New Covenant with better promises.

Today, every believer has the ability to hear the Voice of God. They may not hear Him audibly, but they are absolutely able to discern and hear what the Spirit is saying. Jesus said, "My sheep hear My voice" (John 10:27). That means, if you are born again, you automatically are inclined to hear His voice! That's it! Period.

Still, it is highly important that we understand that there are those who have a higher level of sensitivity, and this is known as the prophetic. Being in the prophetic is something you are either born into or develop through desire and practice.

"That the man of God may be complete, thoroughly equipped for every good work."

– 2 Timothy 3:17

The Word of God (correctly taught) that instructs you about your righteousness in Christ will cause the man of God to be complete! The Gospel you hear preached is correct, but it is not complete until it is working through you! This means, that the Gospel (the finished works of Jesus) working through you is the ultimate sign of maturity.

Jesus loves you and there is nothing you can do about it!

I hope you received encouragement to continue your journey with the Voice of God, no matter the obstacles or delays. The Voice of God is speaking to you right now, saying, "I love you! Follow me!"

You are the best person God has placed wherever you are. Keep following God. Your journey has only begun!

---

[i] *"So when the woman saw that the tree was good for food, that it was pleasant to the eyes, and a tree desirable to make one wise, she took of its fruit and ate. She also gave to her husband with her, and he ate."* – Genesis 3:6

"And Adam was not deceived, but the woman being deceived, fell into transgression." – 1 Timothy 2:14

.

Made in the
USA
Columbia, SC